W9-DFY-362

BAPTIST YOUNG PEOPLE'S UNION
ADMINISTRATION

Baptist
Young People's Union
Administration

ARTHUR FLAKE

Revised in 1942 by J. E. Lambdin
Revised in 1952 by R. Maines Rawls

Convention Press

NASHVILLE TENNESSEE

Printed in the United States of America

10. D 56 R.R.D.

DEDICATED TO THE
BAPTIST YOUNG PEOPLE'S UNION
OF THE BAPTIST CHURCH
WINONA, MISSISSIPPI

This volume is affectionately dedicated, in token of the deepest
gratitude of my heart for the training and development
received at the very beginning of my Christian
life while a member of that Baptist
Young People's Union.

12 23

About the Author

ARTHUR FLAKE (1862-1952) spent his boyhood in Temple, Texas, and was educated in the schools of Bell County and South Belton Institute. He was a successful businessman in Winona, Mississippi, and was an active layman in the Baptist Church there. In 1895 he organized and became president of the first B.Y.P.U. ever organized in Mississippi. He left the business world in 1909 to become a field worker for the Sunday School Board. He gave his time entirely to the B.Y. P.U. work of the Board from 1912 to 1918, during which time he helped to develop the group plan of organization and the methods which are still followed in the unions of the Training Union. He was secretary of the Department of Sunday School Administration of the Sunday School Board for seventeen years, from 1918 to 1936. During these years he wrote eight books on Sunday school administration which revolutionized Southern Baptist Sunday school work. He retired in June, 1936, to his home in Memphis, Tennessee, where he died July 3, 1952.

Contents

A Word of Appreciation

MR. ARTHUR FLAKE, the author of this book, led many young people to dedicate their lives in special Christian service. He was the first man to suggest to the writer of these words that he should devote his life to Baptist Young People's Union work. This took place in Knoxville, Tennessee, in 1914, during the first city Baptist Young People's Union training school ever held in that city, in which Mr. Flake was teaching the *Senior Manual*. The definite decision was made two years later, at Tennessee's first State Baptist Young People's Union Convention, in Chattanooga. Because of this I thank the Lord for Mr. Flake. He continued to the day of his death to be a source of the richest inspiration in my life.

In addition to this personal appreciation of Mr. Flake, I am profoundly grateful on behalf of our Baptist young people, that he gave us this book. It is the fruit of his long years of experience in the field of practical Training Union and Sunday school work. He was a worker with young people and at the same time a close student of all the problems with which we have to deal in that work.

Every Young People's union in the Convention should study this book. It gives a more thorough and exhaustive study of the work of officers and committees than is found in the *Young People's Union Manual*. A faithful application of the methods outlined here will solve Young People's union problems in the most difficult situations. Any church that is thoroughly imbued with the conception of Young People's union work given here, and follows closely these plans, will assuredly make a glorious success of the business of training young Christians in church membership.

J. E. LAMBDIN
Secretary, Training Union Department

Introduction to First Edition

A NEW BOOK of methods for the Baptist Young People's Union awakens unusual interest. The Baptist Young People's Union field has not been overrun with books of methods, since in this department the methods of acknowledged value were accepted and brought into the Standard years ago. Baptist Young People's Union workers of long experience agree that the Baptist Young People's Union ministers to a limited constituency, if successful, and cannot rightly cover a field as large as that of the Sunday school, for example. Therefore, the appearance of a new book of Baptist Young People's Union methods at once provokes the inquiry, What will I find in this book? Is this writer a theorist, trying to "put over" ideas that are interesting but impractical? Or is he a copyist, just writing a book, getting ideas from others, and veiling them by slightly changing certain phrases or applications? Or is he presenting methods which he has tested out through years of patient effort? Has the writer, along with others, found these methods to be valuable and therefore worthy to be passed on?

It is a genuine pleasure to state that Mr. Flake's book falls wholly under the last classification. Mr. Flake was a pioneer Baptist Young People's Union worker among Southern Baptists and has tested, in every detail, the methods he suggests. He organized the Mississippi Baptist Young People's Union State Convention and was its president until it was merged into the State Encampment, as assemblies were called years ago. In his own church he was the leader of Baptist Young People's Union work from the beginning and, indeed, it was from the work of his union that many methods in the *Baptist Young People's Union Manual* were gotten. In 1909,

Mr. Flake became a field secretary of the Sunday School Board. For the first three years he majored in Sunday school work. He then became field secretary of the Baptist Young People's Union work east of the Mississippi River, and propagated Baptist Young People's Union methods with great success throughout the southern states, doing more than any one else to unify methods and put the Standard of Excellence solidly underneath the Baptist Young People's Union work of our Convention. He therefore knows the subject of which he writes, having had practical experience every inch of the way, both as a leader in his own church and as an eminently successful field worker throughout the bounds of the Convention.

We bespeak for this book an enthusiastic reception by training classes and individuals, and urge every officer and committeeman to master it for the sake of the material in it, and in order to secure the recognition it brings in our new course of study called "Baptist Young People's Union Administration."

L. P. LEAVELL
Late Secretary and Editor,
Baptist Young People's Union Department

CHAPTER 1

The Meaning and Aim
of the Baptist
Young People's Union

I. The Meaning of the Baptist Young People's Union

1. *The Baptist Young People's Union a Denominational Organization*

The Baptist Young People's Union is distinctively a denominational agency. The name indicates this. Baptists cannot delegate to nondenominational agencies the task of educating and training their young people, and, in return, expect to receive intelligent, staunch, loyal Baptist church members. Our Baptist leaders realized this and founded the training organization for the express purpose of giving our Baptist church members a thorough, distinctive denominational education and training.

In order to set this matter out clearly, let us notice some characteristics that should mark the finished product of the Baptist Young People's Union.

(1) *Consecrated, useful Christians.*—Certainly the experience gained in the Young People's union should result in producing a finer, better type of Christian. A really intelligent Baptist cannot be narrow and unsympathetic. He will necessarily manifest, in his daily walk and conversation, the spirit of Christ. A true Baptist will unconsciously reflect in his conduct the Christian's graces—faith, virtue, knowledge, self-control, brotherly kindness,

liberality, hospitality, and other fruits of the Spirit. The Young People's union seeks to inculcate in the lives of its members purity in thought, word, and deed.

The Young People's union also seeks to lead young people toward unselfish service to others. It affords them opportunities to give expression to the Christian desire to do good, which desire was implanted within their hearts by the Holy Spirit when Christ was formed in them "the hope of glory."

The Young People's union seeks to nurture and cultivate in the young people the Christ-life, helping them to "manifest the excellencies of Christ" in holy living and helpful deeds.

"But ye are a chosen generation; a royal priesthood, an holy nation, a peculiar people; that ye should shew forth the praises of him who hath called you out of darkness into his marvellous light" (1 Peter 2:9).

Another desirable product of the Baptist Young People's Union is:

(2) *Intelligent, efficient church members.*—One's church membership should be held intensely sacred. The privileges of church membership cannot be prized too highly. This privilege is often held all too lightly. In some quarters the idea of church membership is belittled and discredited. Conditions of entrance into its holy relationships are obscured and mean nothing. Change in habits of life and personal conduct after one becomes a church member is often not in evidence.

Dr. J. M. Frost, of hallowed memory, in *Our Church Life,** aptly says in this connection: "Membership in the church is full of meaning; it is of exceptional honor, and calls for the noblest life. . . . We have never yet realized the full meaning of the honor and distinctions or the responsibility and opportunity of membership in the church of Christ. . . . We honor Christ by honoring his church. We bless the world in making a membership that is commensurate with its high station."

*Out of print.

Practically all our opportunities for service come to us through our church membership. Our greatest usefulness as Christians finds truest expression through our church membership. In our church we link ourselves up with others in co-operative endeavor. Working alone, we would be able to accomplish little, but working together with others, in our church relation, our limited talents, our small fragments of time, our meager offerings, are made powerful and far-reaching in effects and results. Thus each member shares in all the work of his church; in what it does in winning the lost to Christ at home and in giving the gospel to those in foreign lands through our missionaries. The Young People's union seeks to impress upon our Baptist young people the true meaning of their high privileges as church members, magnifying the church of Christ as a divine agency through which and by which men are to be won to God through Christ.

In the Young People's union the young people study how to work together as church members, practicing doing those things which will culminate in their becoming intelligent and efficient members of their churches.

(3) *Loyal, staunch Baptists.*—Baptists are not to blame for the divisions existing among Christians. They are not responsible for the great multiplicity of denominations among Christians today. This divided condition is a source of grief and pain to every thinking, intelligent, loyal Baptist, and all such should pray and work for Christian union on a scriptural basis, as indeed there cannot be a real union on any other ground.

The object of the Young People's union is to teach our Baptist young people what Baptists believe according to the Scriptures, to instil in them true Baptist principles, and to acquaint them with the glorious history of Baptists from New Testament times to the present good hour. The Young People's union seeks to climax its work in the production of Baptists who know why they are Baptists and who can, and will, when occasions arise, give a reason for their faith.

2. *The Baptist Young People's Union a Young People's Organization*

The Baptist Young People's Union is distinctively a young people's organization. It draws its members from the young members of Baptist churches, seventeen to twenty-four years of age. The topics for the weekly meetings and the educational activities are selected and arranged to meet the needs of these young people. The plan of organization and methods of work are adapted to the tastes of young people. The members should plan and conduct their own affairs, co-operating at all times with the director of the Baptist Training Union.

It is understood that the membership is divided into two classes: active and associate.

(1) *Active.*—The active members are those who have made a public profession of faith in Christ and united with a Baptist church.

(2) *Associate.*—This group is composed of young people who are not members of Baptist churches. These are always gladly welcomed to all the privileges of the union except holding office and voting. It is tacitly understood that a union will not seek to build up its membership with associate members.

3. *The Baptist Young People's Union a Soul-Winning Organization*

The Baptist Young People's Union is essentially a soul-winning agency. It is evangelistic in purpose. One of its chief aims is to train the young people in soul-winning.

The weekly meetings with the programs based upon the topics are not primarily soul-winning meetings in the sense that special effort is made at these meetings to induce lost people to accept Christ. Occasionally, certainly, the weekly meetings should be given this turn. The president and the leader of the meeting should plan the program, and the topics should be developed with a view to making a public appeal to the associate members of the union who are not saved to accept and publicly to confess Christ as their Saviour.

Also, in unions where there are a number of young people who are not Christians, at the close of the meeting, the president should use a few minutes to press home upon their hearts the claims of Christ and urge them to confess him. Also, when visitors are present this should be done.

Primarily, the Baptist Young People's Union is a training school for the purpose of training soul-winners rather than an enlistment agency.

The preaching services and the Sunday school have as their supreme business the work of enlisting soldiers in the Lord's army. The Baptist Young People's Union has as its supreme business the work of training these newly enlisted recruits to be good soldiers of Christ.

A Baptist Young People's Union in a Baptist church stands for the great truth that one of the best ways to win more souls is to train more soul-winners. The Baptist Young People's Union is a training school in evangelism, training its young church members in praying for the lost, in speaking personally to the lost, and in the use of their Bibles in winning the lost to Christ.

4. *The Baptist Young People's Union a Missionary Organization*

This does not mean that the Baptist Young People's Union is a money-gathering agency for the purpose of supporting missionaries or other work of a missionary nature, independent of the church. That is not so. The Baptist Young People's Union is not a money-raising institution. It is a missionary teaching, a missionary training, a missionary enlistment agency. Let us see what is meant by this:

First, the young people are brought face to face with a needy, lost world.

Second, the young people are given the missionary message of the Bible.

Third, the young people learn the history of the missionary achievements.

Fourth, the young people are enlisted to give of their means to send the gospel to all nations.

Fifth, the young people are enlisted to give themselves to go where God calls and directs.

(1) *Face to face with a lost world.*—In the Baptist Young People's Union the young people learn that "the whole world lieth in wickedness" (1 John 5:19); that the supreme need of every man is Christ; that all men everywhere are lost—the Gentile, Jew, heathen, the white man, black man, red man, yellow man, the rich and poor, the wise and ignorant; that all stand condemned before God, and that their only hope is in Christ.

Young people who have had their training in the Baptist Young People's Union do not ask the oft-heard heart-sickening questions, "Are the heathen lost who never heard the gospel message?" "Will the heathen have another chance after this life?" and similar questions.

The young people who have been trained in the Baptist Young People's Union know that Christ died for the world, that "all have sinned, and come short of the glory of God."

"As it is written, There is none righteous, no, not one: there is none that understandeth, there is none that seeketh after God. They are all gone out of the way, they are together become unprofitable: there is none that doeth good, no, not one. Their throat is an open sepulchre; with their tongues they have used deceit; the poison of asps is under their lips: whose mouth is full of cursing and bitterness: their feet are swift to shed blood: destruction and misery are in their ways: and the way of peace have they not known: there is no fear of God before their eyes" (Rom. 3:10–18).

(2) *The missionary message of the Bible.*—In the Baptist Young People's Union the young people learn that they are partners with Christ in giving the good news to the lost of earth; that they are to continue the

work that he began in person and trained his immediate followers to do. They take seriously the words of Jesus when he said, "Peace be unto you: as my Father hath sent me, even so send I you" (John 20:21). Young Baptists who have had proper training believe that the Great Commission is the Christian's marching order. They take to heart the words of Christ when he said: "All power is given unto me in heaven and in earth. Go ye therefore, and teach all nations, baptizing them in the name of the Father, and of the Son, and of the Holy Ghost: teaching them to observe all things whatsoever I have commanded you: and, lo, I am with you alway, even unto the end of the world" (Matt. 28:18–20).

The Baptist Young People's Union is an active missionary agency whose business is to teach and to train the young people that the churches of Christ are the divinely-appointed means for carrying out our Lord's last command to give the whole gospel to the whole world.

(3) *History of missionary achievement.*—Wherever the missionary has gone, Christ, true to his promise, "Lo, I am with you," has gone. Christ was with the apostle Paul in all his missionary journeys; Christ was with Carey in India, with Judson in Burma, with Livingstone and Moffat in Africa, with Paton in the South Sea Islands, with Yates and Hartwell in China, with Hart in Argentina. These men have all said that Christ was with them. Likewise, any man or woman from the days of the apostle Paul up to this time, who has not counted his life dear unto himself, but has taken Christ at his word and given his life to Christ in service, no matter where, bears testimony to the fact that Christ was with him all the way. The history of missions is a history of wonderful achievement. The most successful enterprise known to the world is the missionary enterprise. The most thrilling stories ever heard have been told by Christ's missionaries in recounting Christ's dealing with them and through them.

There are no biographies comparable to those of Carey,

Judson, Ann of Ava, Livingstone, Paton, and hundreds of others of Christ's missionaries.

The Baptist Young People's Union is full of missions. A missionary topic is studied once each month. The members of the union study missions twelve weeks each year. They keep in touch with the onward progress of the kingdom of God through the work of the missionaries.

(4) *Give of their means.*—In the Baptist Young People's Union the young people learn what God would have them do with their money. In the union the young people get the extremely practical lesson that money is as essential as man in giving the gospel to the world.

"For there is no difference between the Jew and the Greek: for the same Lord over all is rich unto all that call upon him. For whosoever shall call upon the name of the Lord shall be saved. How then shall they call on him in whom they have not believed? and how shall they believe in him of whom they have not heard? and how shall they hear without a preacher? and how shall they preach, except they be sent? as it is written, How beautiful are the feet of them that preach the gospel of peace, and bring glad tidings of good things!" (Rom. 10:12–15). The young people are taught the Bible standard of giving. They are not taught to give of their means "what they feel they ought to give" or "until it hurts" or "according to the needs of the field," but proportionately.

Then each young church member is enlisted definitely to co-operate with his church in supporting all the causes fostered by the denomination by making contributions to these objects through his church.

(5) *Give themselves.*—Only young people make missionaries. No others are accepted by the Boards. Even people of early maturity are not eligible for missionary service. Our hope of winning the world is our young people. The Young People's union seeks to lead them to consecrate themselves to Christ's cause and yield to Christ's call to go wherever he shall direct. While they stand, hesitant as to which road to take, the Young Peo-

ple's union points them to a life of service for Christ and calls insistently upon them to decide for him and his cause as over against the call of the world to a life of selfishness and ease. Multitudes have responded to this call and answered, "Here am I; send me," and today we witness the glorious spectacle of hundreds of our finest and best young men and women standing ready to go.

5. The Baptist Young People's Union
a Social Organization

Through the Young People's union the church may conserve, in a practical way, the entire life of its young members: the spiritual, mental, and social. The social natures of young people crave fellowship. In the Young People's union this desire is met in a fine way. How much better it is for a church to provide social pleasures for the young people under the proper auspices than for the young people to satisfy these longings in an atmosphere unfriendly to their spiritual welfare!

The church should plan social meetings as well as prayer meetings for its young people. This it does through and in the Young People's union. Each union should plan its social life on the basis of the social needs and desires of its members. It should always be distinctly Christian. Thus the play-life, as well as the prayer-life, of the members of Baptist churches is taken care of.

6. The Baptist Young People's Union
a Church Organization

This means that the Young People's union, as a vital part of the Training Union, is fostered and supported by the church. The church assumes entire responsibility for the education and training of its members. It should furnish each union a suitable place in which to meet and all the materials and supplies needed to carry on the work effectively. The church should finance the work, buying the study course books, defraying the expenses of the socials, equipping and maintaining a library.

Large churches are employing directors who devote their entire time to developing the Baptist Training Union. Those in the churches having chief responsibility in this matter are:

(1) *The pastor.*—The pastor is the shepherd ministering to the spiritual needs of the members of the church, guarding them from temptation, and warning them against all kinds of danger and pitfalls. The pastor is also the "overseer" of the people, planning for their development and usefulness and keeping them busy at worthwhile tasks. He should see that the church elects a director for the Training Union.

(2) *The Sunday school superintendent.*—The superintendent of the Sunday school should link up with the pastor and aid him in planning for the training of the church members. He should help find a director wherever one is needed. The superintendent is usually a man of influence in the church. There is no place where his influence will count for more to the cause of Christ than to use it in a substantial way in behalf of the members of his church.

From among the members of the Young People's union and the Adult union the sympathetic, vigilant, aggressive Sunday school superintendent will be able, in a short time, to secure all the additional officers and teachers needed for the Sunday school.

The live Sunday school superintendent will not sit and wring his hands and idly wish for consecrated, intelligent Sunday school officers and teachers. He will get into intimate personal touch with the Young People's union and with the members of the Adult union and cooperate with the pastor and leaders of the Training Union in training and developing a corps of Sunday school officers and teachers upon whom he can depend.

(3) *The deacons.*—Deacons in Baptist churches occupy enviable positions. "For they that have used the office of a deacon well purchase to themselves a good degree, and great boldness in the faith which is in Christ Jesus"

(1 Tim. 3:13). In no place can the deacons serve better than in helping to develop a great Training Union in the church.

A FENCE OR AN AMBULANCE

'Twas a dangerous cliff, as they freely confessed,
    Though to walk near its crest was so pleasant;
But over its terrible edge there had slipped
    A duke and full many a peasant.
So the people said something would have to be done,
    But their projects did not at all tally;
Some said, "Put a fence around the edge of the cliff,"
    Some, "An ambulance down in the valley."

    . . . .

But the cry for the ambulance carried the day,
    For it spread through the neighboring city;
A fence may be useful or not, it is true,
    But each heart became brimful of pity
For those who slipped over that dangerous cliff;
    And the dwellers in highway and alley
Gave pounds or gave pence, not to put up a fence,
    But an ambulance down in the valley.

    . . . .

Then an old sage remarked: "It's a marvel to me
    That people give far more attention
To repairing results than to stopping the cause,
    When they'd much better aim at prevention.
Let us stop at its source all this mischief," cried he,
    "Come, neighbors and friends, let us rally;
If the cliff we will fence we might almost dispense
    With the ambulance down in the valley."

    . . . .

Better guide well the young than reclaim them when old,
    For the voice of true wisdom is calling,
"To rescue the fallen is good, but 'tis best
    To prevent other people from falling."
Better close up the source of temptation and crime
    Than deliver from dungeon or galley;
Better put a strong fence round the top of the cliff
    Than an ambulance down in the valley.

                   —JOSEPH MALINS

II. The Aim of the Baptist Young People's Union

"That our sons may be as plants grown up in their youth; that our daughters may be as corner stones, polished after the similitude of a palace" (Psalm 144:12).

The aim of the Baptist Young People's Union is to train its members in the duties and privileges of church membership. This aim finds attractive expression in the brief and popular slogan "Training in Church Membership."

It is the purpose in this study to consider some simple, practical things which are involved in one's church membership, some of the means to be employed, and processes through which he must come in order to be a church member of the greatest usefulness.

What are some of the things every member of a Baptist church should know and do? Let us deal with this vital matter in a definite, practical, and simple manner.

1. Church Members Should Pray

There is no such thing as living a happy, useful, victorious life in Christ apart from prayer. It is essential that one should begin the new life in Christ in the right way by giving attention to the cultivation of his prayer life. The normal Christian life is the life in which prayer is the daily habit. This habit must be cultivated. It will not, cannot, thrive on neglect.

The time to begin the cultivation of this most important habit is when young. The Young People's union seeks to train its members to

(1) *Cultivate the habit of daily secret prayer.*—The Young People's union enjoins upon the young people the need and importance of secret prayer, and encourages them to form the habit of daily private devotion. The young people form prayer bands and make prayer pacts, agreeing to pray daily. They agree on special objects for which to pray and thus prayer becomes a real means by which they confidently expect to accomplish certain heartfelt desires and worthy aims otherwise unattainable.

(2) *Lead in public prayer.*—It is vastly important that church members shall form the habit of leading in public prayer. Many otherwise useful Christians evade this duty, claiming that they have not the "prayer gift." The difficulty is the gift was neglected in their early Christian experience and they have allowed themselves to be cheated out of one of the greatest privileges ever vouchsafed to a child of God. Oh, the safeguard to the young Christian to stand or kneel among his fellow young Christians and lead them in talking to the Father! This habit of leading in public prayer is a means of spiritual growth also. It should be indulged in and cultivated by all Christians, both young and old.

An important part of the work of the Young People's union is to get its members to lead in public prayer and thus enjoy one of the greatest of all Christian privileges.

2. *Church Members Should Study Their Bibles*

This privilege and duty goes hand in hand with that of prayer. Tragic beyond expression is the life of the Christian when prayer and Bible study are neglected. The Christian life—the new life—must be nurtured. The Christian—the new man—must be fed or he will cease to thrive and grow. His is a spiritual life which must be maintained and built up by taking in spiritual food. Prayer and Bible study are two of the chief elements in the spiritual diet. The neglect of either of these elements means spiritual decline.

Here we have the Bible close at hand. Whenever we will, we can open its pages and refresh our souls. It is both food and drink to the hungry, thirsty soul.

One main business of the Young People's union is to create and cultivate a love for God's Word in the hearts and minds of the young people. Another is to help the young people to form the habit of daily Bible reading early in their Christian experience, with the hope that the habit will continue through life. The Young People's union seeks to get the young people to *study* their Bibles.

The Daily Bible Readers' Course and the Bible courses in the study course books are specially provided with this end in view.

3. *Church Members Should Speak Publicly for Christ*

While the Christian life is pre-eminently a life of action, of deeds and not words, yet public testimony and public speaking for Christ have an important place in the development and work of the child of God.

(1) *We owe it to Christ.*—Think, if possible, of one's being saved from an awful death, and never publicly thanking his rescuer for saving him. Think of one thus saved sitting quietly in a congregation, while others who have been saved are telling about their Saviour.

Yes, we owe it to Christ to testify publicly, in words of praise and adoration, of his goodness and mercy in saving us. The psalmist said, "Bless the Lord, O my soul: and all that is within me, bless his holy name." Some mature church members claim they cannot do this. They say they are not gifted in speech, they are not trained public speakers. Their tongues cleave to the roof of their mouths when they try to speak publicly for Christ; their knees smite together mightily. What they need is the opportunity which is afforded in the Young People's union for learning to talk for Christ. They were not born into the kingdom of God dumb. They came in with joy in their souls and a shout of praise on their lips. But they have neglected the duty of praise to God so long it seems now impossible to begin.

(2) *An encouragement to other Christians.*—"The Lord God hath given me the tongue of the learned, that I should know how to speak a word in season to him that is weary: he wakeneth morning by morning, he wakeneth mine ear to hear as the learned" (Isa. 50:4). Christians should stand and speak publicly for Christ as an encouragement to their fellow Christians. The Christian lives in an alien world—far from home—in a beautiful, charming, attractive world, to be sure, but nevertheless

in a world unfriendly to Christ and to the people of Christ. They get downhearted and discouraged amid the turmoil and strife on every hand. They need the encouragement of their fellow Christians. For this reason every child of God should be glad to proclaim to the world his allegiance to Christ, his hope in the resurrection, and his hope in a better world in which peace and righteousness shall reign. "Then they that feared the Lord spake often one to another" (Mal. 3:16).

(3) *An influence upon sinners to accept Christ.*—Many a lost man has found Christ as a result of the testimony of some earnest child of God. This ability and duty to stand and speak for Christ is of great importance in the life of the Christian. The sinner is not satisfied with his condition; he is restless and ill at ease; there is that within his soul calling for something, he knows not what. It should be a joy for those who know Christ to proclaim what he has done for them, and do it so effectively that sinners shall desire Christ and accept him.

(4) *A means of growth in grace.*—The more one tells of what Christ has done for him the stronger his faith becomes. Public testimony means growth in grace—a strengthening of one's faith, an increasing love for Christ, and an increasing desire to see others saved and the world made better.

4. *Church Members Should Be Soul-Winners*

Every child of God should be a soul-winner. A church with one hundred members should have one hundred soul-winners. A church with one thousand members should have one thousand soul-winners. A church with five thousand members should have five thousand soul-winners. Think of a church of one hundred members, every one of the hundred members busy winning souls! Think of a church of one thousand members, each member busy winning souls! Think of a church of five thousand members, each member busy winning souls! The very thought fires the imagination and mightily stirs the soul. "I will make you fishers of men," is a personal word of Christ to every saved man. A church membership properly trained would mean a church membership of soul-winners. Some things that hinder the love of Christ from flowing through us to the lost all around about us are: the pleasures of the world; the cares of the world; the deceitfulness of riches; the exceeding sinfulness of sin. It was the same way in the early days of Christianity. Like conditions prevailed then as now, yet, "they went forth, and preached every where." Not only the preachers—but the entire membership!

5. Church Members Should Contribute of Their Means Scripturally

All church members are included here. System and not spasm should be the plan. What is meant by "scriptural giving"? Let the Scripture answer, "Upon the first day of the week let every one of you lay by him in store, as God hath prospered him." The well-trained church member will meet this Bible requirement cheerfully. An early beginning is necessary.

6. Church Members Should Have Doctrinal Stamina

They should know truth from error, and have the courage to contend for the truth, and resist error no matter where found. "That we henceforth be no more children, tossed to and fro, and carried about with every wind of doctrine, by the sleight of men, and cunning craftiness, whereby they lie in wait to deceive" (Eph. 4:14). Members of Baptist churches should believe something and stand for what they believe the Scriptures teach.

7. Church Members Should Prepare Themselves for Special Service

There are many places of service in the churches requiring trained workers. There are enough tasks to go around. There need not be one idler in any church. However, the members need to be prepared, each one for his individual work.

(1) *The Sunday school.*—In this great organization there are scores of places needing men and women of executive ability and teaching qualifications. These strategic positions must be filled by the members of the church from all walks, trades, and professions. All members should seek to prepare themselves in a definite way for the most intelligent and effective service possible.

Being a member of the Sunday school should be taken as a duty by every church member and each one should gladly welcome an opportunity to prepare himself and assiduously set himself to the task.

(2) *Deacons.*—Special preparation is required to succeed here, as it is in every great undertaking. Deacons are usually good men, among the best in the churches. They are usually among the most intelligent and successful businessmen in the churches. But in the matter of leadership in successful church administration they may be just beginners. In many instances they have not prepared themselves for this work. They do not know their business. The Training Union can be an invaluable aid here!

(3) *W. M. U. leaders.*—The Woman's Missionary Union has distinguished itself by securing intelligent leadership. Its continued success depends upon maintaining this type of leadership. This, of course, calls for a program of training to which the Training Union has dedicated itself.

(4) *Missionaries.*—From our young church membership must come all our missionaries. There should be a definite program to enlist our brightest young men and women in the great missionary enterprise. We should pray and expect our best to give themselves to go wherever God may direct. Special preparation is needful here at the very beginning of the Christian experience of our young people.

(5) *Preachers.*—Churches should be at the task by

precept and prayer, calling out the best young men we have to consecrate themselves definitely to the work of the ministry. Early training is essential here.

IN CONCLUSION

We submit that it is both desirable and practicable for church members to engage in the activities set out in the foregoing discussion. Furthermore, we contend the future hope for the progress of Baptist churches is dependent upon the members doing these things, and that these things are absolutely essential to our life as a Baptist people and to the onward march of the kingdom of God in the world.

The aim of the Young People's union is to produce church members who will do these things. Its weekly programs, study courses, and schedules of activities are all designed to train the young Christian by giving him practice in doing these things. It has already wrought gloriously in our church and denominational life, and now occupies a pre-eminent place as our agency for training young Christians in church membership.

OUTLINE

I. THE MEANING OF THE BAPTIST YOUNG PEOPLE'S UNION

1. The Baptist Young People's Union a Denominational Organization

2. The Baptist Young People's Union a Young People's Organization

3. The Baptist Young People's Union a Soul-Winning Organization

4. The Baptist Young People's Union a Missionary Organization

5. The Baptist Young People's Union a Social Organization

6. The Baptist Young People's Union a Church Organization

II. THE AIM OF THE BAPTIST YOUNG PEOPLE'S UNION

1. Church Members Should Pray
2. Church Members Should Study Their Bibles
3. Church Members Should Speak Publicly for Christ
4. Church Members Should Be Soul-Winners
5. Church Members Should Contribute of Their Means Scripturally
6. Church Members Should Have Doctrinal Stamina
7. Church Members Should Prepare Themselves for Special Service

CHAPTER 2

Organizing the Baptist Young People's Union

I. FOLLOW THE STANDARD OF EXCELLENCE—THE TRAINING GUIDE OF THE BAPTIST YOUNG PEOPLE'S UNION

Suggested by the Sunday School Board of the Southern Baptist Convention. Effective first quarter, 1952.

(Note.—The ages of the Young People's union are 17–24, inclusive.)

I. ORGANIZATION

1. *Officers.*—President, vice-president, secretary, group captains, social leader, missionary leader, and Bible readers' leader. An adult counselor is recommended. (Song leader and pianist recommended if needed.) All officers shall be members of a Baptist church. Each officer shall be instructed in his duties at the beginning of his term of office. The counselor, president, and at least four other officers shall hold, or earn during the quarter, an award on BAPTIST YOUNG PEOPLE'S UNION ADMINISTRATION.

President Responsible

2. *Committees.*—Program, membership, social, missionary, and Bible reading. (1) The program committee shall meet each month to plan the programs for the weekly meetings. (2) The other committee chairmen

20

I. ORGANIZATION—*Continued*

shall direct the work of their committee members through monthly committee meetings or individual assignments.

3. *Groups.*—The union shall be divided into groups, each with a group captain.

II. MEETINGS

1. *Weekly Meeting.*—The union shall conduct a weekly meeting, with program based upon materials in *Baptist Young People* or *Baptist Married Young People,* published by the Baptist Sunday School Board. (1) Every active (Baptist) member shall participate in the program at least twice a quarter. (2) Reading from the quarterly cannot be counted as taking part on the program.

President and Program Committee Responsible

2. *Officers' Council.*—The officers of the union shall meet monthly to review the work of the union and make plans for the next month. (1) The union shall co-operate with the Training Union in its plan for the officers' council. (2) The secretary shall make a written report of the work of the union for the past month. (3) The other officers shall present written plans for the coming month. (4) The president shall make a monthly written report to the department director if the department is organized; otherwise, to the executive committee of the Training Union.

President Responsible

III. ACTIVITIES

1. *Study.*—(1) *Lesson Course.*— The union shall follow the lesson course in *Baptist Young People* or *Baptist Married Young People,* published by the Baptist Sunday School Board. (2) *Textbook Study Course.* —The union shall take at least one study course every twelve months, using a book of the Graded Training Union Study Course of the Baptist Sunday School Board.

President and Program Committee Responsible

2. *Daily Bible Reading and Prayer.* —The union shall follow the course for individual daily Bible reading and daily prayer as outlined in *Baptist Young People* or *Baptist Married Young People* and conduct a weekly review (Bible drill) on the readings.

Bible Readers' Leader and Bible Reading Committee Responsible

3. *Worship.*—(1) The union shall promote attendance upon the evening preaching service. (2) The union shall promote attendance upon the weekly prayer meeting of the church.

Vice-President and Membership Committee Responsible

(3) The union shall promote daily family worship in every home represented, using the daily readings of the Uniform Sunday School Lessons.

Bible Readers' Leader and Bible Reading Committee Responsible

4. *Stewardship and Missions.*—(1) The union shall promote education in stewardship, tithing, and systematic giving by all its members to church expenses, benevolences, and missions, according to the church plan. (2) The union shall encourage the enlistment of all its members in active service in other church activi-

Missionary Leader and Missionary Committee Responsible

III. ACTIVITIES—*Continued*

ties and organizations. (3) The union shall take part each quarter in some practical missionary activity. (4) Every active member shall be urged to pray for and witness to lost people daily.

5. *Social Life.*—The union shall have at least one social each quarter. Combination socials, held with the Sunday school classes or other church organizations, may be recognized not more than twice a year as meeting this requirement.

> Social Leader and Social Committee Responsible

6. *Visitation.*—Regular visitation of all absentees and prospects shall be sponsored.

> Vice-President and Membership Committee Responsible

IV. ACHIEVEMENT

1. The union shall encourage every member to make a high grade on the Eight Point Record System.
2. The weekly average number of members making 70 per cent or above [1] shall be at least two-thirds of the weekly average enrolment.[2]

> President and All Officers Responsible

Note.—If the union has reached the points on this Standard for a quarter, application for the Standard award should be made in duplicate to the state Training Union secretary on forms furnished by him. To the union qualifying as Standard, the quarterly Standard award will be sent by the Baptist Sunday School Board.

Each union should send the names and addresses of its president and counselor to the state Training Union department after each election of officers.

[1] Add the weekly totals of members making 70 per cent or above and divide the sum by the number of Sundays in the quarter.
[2] Add the weekly enrolments and divide the sum by the number of Sundays in the quarter.

II. How to Organize the Baptist Young People's Union

The organization as outlined in the Standard should be set up in every Young People's union.

1. *Officers*

The officers of a Baptist Young People's Union are as follows: president, vice-president, secretary, social leader, missionary leader, Bible readers' leader, and group captains. A song leader and a pianist are also recommended to all unions which have musical instruments in the meeting rooms. Every Young People's union should have an adult counselor, who is elected annually by the church. A good counselor should serve indefinitely.

Let us see the best method of electing officers and how long they should serve.

(1) *Term of office.*—It is generally agreed that the election of officers should be semiannual, thus limiting the term of service of the officers to six months. The terms should run from October 1 to March 31, and from April 1 to September 30. These periods are recommended because annual Promotion Day comes the last Sunday in September. The custom of electing officers semiannually has two points of value to recommend it.

a. Good officers may be re-elected.—The semiannual custom of electing officers does not mean that faithful, efficient officers may not be re-elected. They may. However, they should not be continued in office indefinitely. Often the impression prevails that the present officers are the only members of the union capable of making efficient officers and the semiannual election is only a matter of form—the report of the nominating committee reading as follows: "We, your committee on nominations, recommend that the present officers of the union be elected for another term," and so forth. There are two ill effects usually resulting from doing it this way. Those in office are apt to get the impression that the offices belong to them, and other capable young people become discouraged and lose interest in the work, because of a monopoly on the offices of the union. It is a good idea to re-elect an efficient officer for a second term when there is a scarcity of suitable available material for the office, and when a change might jeopardize the best interests of the union.

b. Inefficient officers eliminated.—The short term is valuable in that it gives the union an opportunity to get rid of unfaithful, inefficient officers before the work of the union has suffered beyond repair. Good officers may be elected for a second term, but officers who will not study the work and attend to their duties should under no circumstances be re-elected.

(2) Method of electing officers

a. Electing the president.—It is usually best to have a nominating committee of three members besides the counselor, who is by virtue of his position a member of all the committees. This committee should select and nominate the president perhaps a month to six weeks in advance of the time he takes office. This will allow sufficient time for the incoming president to make a study of the entire situation and thus be able to work with the nominating committee intelligently in the selection of his comrades.

b. Electing the other officers.—The president-elect should immediately acquaint himself thoroughly with the duties of each officer and committee of the union. He should also make a study of the members of the union personally and thus be able to assist the nominating committee in the selection and proper adjustment of the new organization. An outline of the duties of the officers of the union would serve as a splendid guide to the nominating committee in selecting the officers.

(3) Avoiding mistakes.

—How often do we find misfits among the officers of a union! A vice-president unsuited to his task; a secretary unfit for his work; a missionary leader wholly without the necessary qualifications for his duties; "square pegs in round holes," so to speak! How may these mistakes be avoided?

In addition to the precaution contained in the method of electing the officers suggested above, let the nominating committee be much in prayer; let the committee call the union to prayer for divine guidance of the committee in its deliberations. "Pray without ceasing." "If any of you lack wisdom, let him ask of God, that giveth to all men liberally, and upbraideth not; and it shall be given him" (James 1:5).

(4) *Public installation service.*—This service can be made specially attractive, and will prove a great encouragement to the young people in their work. A good program should be arranged. Each one of the new officers should have a place on this program. He should make a thorough study of his duties prior to the installation service. He should tell what these duties are and pledge himself to attend to them faithfully.

Often the pastor is glad to conduct the installation service for the whole Training Union at the evening service, at which time a special program would be presented.

2. *Committees*

In the Baptist Young People's Union the following committees are necessary: membership, social, program, Bible reading, and missionary.

We are so in the habit of having committees for everything that it is doubtful if we understand why the union has these committees. Therefore, let us study briefly what the purpose is in having the above committees and how the committees should be made up.

(1) *Purpose of committees.*—What is the use of committees in the Young People's union? What are committees for? Why have committees, anyway? In a study class on one occasion the question, "Why have committees in the union?" was asked. The following answers were given: "Just because," "We have always had committees," "Oh, we couldn't get along without committees," and "We have

to have committees." All this was given in a tone of voice indicating that committees are simply a necessary evil. These answers all indicate that the real purpose of committees in the Young People's union is not understood. Let us study briefly some of the underlying reasons for having committees in the Young People's union.

a. To get the work of the union done.—What is the work of the Young People's union?

(*a*) All the church members of this age group should be brought into the union and encouraged to be faithful to its program. This is the work of the membership committee.

(*b*) The members of the union should be trained to speak publicly for Christ and to lead in public prayer. This is the work of the program committee.

(*c*) The young people should be led to read a portion of God's Word and to engage in secret prayer every day. This is the work of the Bible reading committee.

(*d*) The missionary education of the young people, and their actual enlistment in giving, should be definitely looked after. This is the work of the missionary committee.

(*e*) A spirit of love, brotherly kindness, and practical helpfulness should be cultivated among the young people. This is the work of the social committee.

b. To develop the young people.—A great word in Young People's union work is "training." The idea of "learning by doing"—developing through exercise—is a Young People's union fundamental. In the doing of the work of the committees, the development of the members, individually, is assured.

Training is inherent in the work of the committees. When the members of the committees do well the work assigned to them, their development is inevitable.

Another purpose in having committees:

c. To train the young people in teamwork.—"The art of living together" is truly a fine art. The art of working together is a finer art. Here unselfishness and intelligence are indissolubly linked; they go hand in hand.

In doing committee work the young people learn to appreciate the opinions of their fellows; they learn to sacrifice individual preference for the larger good. They learn much of the value of a combination of individual resources in working for Christ. They learn how to blend their ideas, opinions, and efforts with others to achieve worthy ends. The well-rounded Christian must get a good part of his education from contact with others. Committee work furnishes the training ground for this most highly valuable part of the education of young church members.

The training to be gained by the young church members in the union, by intelligently serving on committees, is experience greatly needed for the preparation of men for deacons who are able to serve well; for preparation of men for finance committees who know how to administer successfully the financial affairs of the churches; for the preparation of men and women who, when appointed by the pastor to serve on committees, may by their intelligent co-operation and vigorous execution show themselves in deed and in truth "workmen who needeth not to be ashamed."

(2) *Size of committees.*—In a Young People's union the size of the committees is regulated by the plan of organization, the "group plan." If the union has enough members, there should be a member of each committee from each group in addition to the chairman. Thus, a union divided into three groups would have four members on each committee, the chairman and three other members. In smaller unions, the chairman should be the only representative of his committee on his own group. This, of course, does not apply to the program committee which is composed of the president, group captains, and counselor. If the union has a song leader and a pianist, these also serve on the program committee.

(3) *Formation of committees*

a. *Committee chairmen.*—The chairmen of Young People's union committees are:

Program committee—president
Membership committee—vice-president
Social committee—social leader
Missionary committee—missionary leader
Bible reading committee—Bible readers' leader

In electing officers, the nominating committee should take into consideration their qualifications for leading in the work of the committees of which they are to be chairmen.

b. Selecting committee members.—After the officers have been elected, they should meet to select committee members. This should be done by the committee chairmen in co-operation with the group captains, president, and counselor. This group will want to keep in mind that every member of the union should serve either as an officer or on a committee. With this in mind, the union secretary should furnish each officer with a complete list of members.

In this same meeting of officers the union should be divided into groups. After the groups are formed, the committees are set up as follows:

The program committee is already made up, consisting of the president, group captains, song leader, pianist, and counselor.

The vice-president, the chairman of the membership committee, will make up his committee by selecting a member from each group, beginning with group number one.

The social leader, the chairman of the social committee, will make up the social committee in the same way.

The missionary leader, the chairman of the missionary committee, will next make up his committee.

The Bible readers' leader, the chairman of the Bible reading committee, will in like manner make up his committee.

Each chairman will have the help of the counselor, president, group captains, and the other officers in forming his committee, to insure an intelligent distribution of the young people according to their talents and tastes. Each chairman should be given a first choice in one group. New members will receive special attention. All the experienced members will not be grouped together on one or two committees. Special and peculiar characteristics of the different members will be considered. Those who are uncongenial will not be put on the same committee. An intelligent adjustment of the workers to the work will be made. This principle lies at the very foundation of success everywhere.

3. *Groups*

The union should be divided into two, three, or four groups, depending upon the size of the union and the number of prospects assigned to it. Each group should have six or seven members. Each group should have a captain who shall have general oversight of the members and work of the group. Let us consider some reasons for organizing a Young People's union on the group plan.

(1) *Why the group plan*

a. Makes practical the work of the officers and the committees.—Every committee has a member in each group who is charged with making the work of his committee effective in his particular group. Each committeeman thus works in a definite way with six or seven young people instead of trying to work in a haphazard way with a large group. The chairmen of committees also have the group captains with whom they may co-operate in making their work effective.

b. Locates responsibility for each phase of the work.— This is done by having group captains over small groups of six or seven members charged with the development of each member of the group. The group captain should see that every part of the work is carried on in his group. Also there is in each group a committeeman having definite responsibility touching the work of his committee.

c. Provides for the development of all of the mem-

bers.—This is perhaps the chief reason for dividing the union into groups. Before the group plan was adopted only a few of the members were given individual attention by the officers. Only a few were used on the program. Only a few were called on to lead in prayer. Only a few were asked to do anything except listen.

The group plan has changed all this so that now all the members must be used on the program; all must take the study course; all must participate in all the activities of the union; the untrained, the timid, the hesitant, and seemingly incompetent all have their chance. They are not lost in the "crowd." Group captains give them individual attention. Once they were overlooked because they "could not do anything"; now for the same reason they are given special attention.

d. Arouses a fine spirit of friendly rivalry.—There is no doubt that the group plan of organization makes an appeal to the different groups to excel the other groups in accomplishing the different tasks committed to them. Each group doing its work in a worthy manner influences the other groups to emulate its example and even to excel it. Thus the scriptural injunction to "consider one another to provoke unto . . . good works" is carried out.

The officers should always be careful to see that the enthusiasm and rivalry thus created should be of the right sort and kept within the proper bounds.

e. The group plan is successful.—To the truthfulness of this statement thousands of workers over the land can testify. Good programs are being carried out weekly by thousands of unions every Sunday evening. Hundreds of thousands of young people are being trained in unions organized on the group plan. Young people are taking the study courses and reading their Bibles in great numbers.

(2) *How to divide the union into groups.*—Immediately after the installation of the new officers the president should call them together to form the group and appoint the committees, both of which should be done in the same meeting.

One method used widely for doing this is to place the officers in the groups first, putting a committee chairman in each group. Then let each committee chairman choose his committee members, choosing as many as there are groups, and place one member of his committee in each group. Every member of the union should either hold an office or be on some committee. If there are more members than can be given a definite place of service, then create another committee, such as publicity committee, or room committee. (See charts, pp. 34–35.)

Another method for dividing into groups is one by which the officers are placed in the groups first, with a committee chairman in each group. Then the members are distributed, keeping in mind the talents of all. After the groups are properly balanced the committees are appointed. One group at a time should be organized, and a member for each committee appointed in that group before moving on to the next group. Each committee chairman should have a first choice in one group. After the groups are divided and the committees appointed, all necessary adjustments should be made to get the groups and committees properly balanced.

(3) *Names enrolled on the organization chart.*—Immediately following the completion of the organization the secretary should place all names on an organization chart, as shown on the following pages, and place this chart in a conspicuous place in the union room. This shows every member his office or committee at a glance. The secretary may easily make this chart.

III. How to Use the Standard of Excellence as the Training Guide

1. *A Called Meeting of Officers*

The president should call a special meeting of the officers and chairmen of committees for the purpose of considering the matter of using the Standard as the training guide of the union. He should be assured before the meeting that each officer and the chairman of each committee will be in attendance at this meeting. In fact, all the members of each committee and others who may desire to attend should be invited to the meeting. After a brief devotion, in which prayer should play an important part, the president should explain the object of the meeting fully.

2. *The Standard of Excellence Explained*

Tracts setting out the Standards of Excellence should be placed in the hands of each one present and a large Standard should be displayed on the wall. Each point should then be explained by the president and other officers who have been thinking about the matter. An opportunity should be given for expressions on the part of all present, and agreement should be reached that the union will follow the Standard as its training guide.

3. *Each Officer Should Assume Responsibility for His Part*

In this meeting each officer should understand what his part is in making the union Standard, and he should stand and publicly assume responsibility to the union for meeting the requirement for which he is responsible.

4. *Agree upon a Time Limit*

After a thorough discussion of the whole Standard of Excellence situation, this meeting should set a time limit for reaching the Standard of Excellence, and all agree that each will do his best to meet every requirement before the expiration of the time set.

5. *The Union Should Vote to Reach the Standard*

At the very next meeting of the union the president should acquaint the union with the action of the officers and committees concerning the Standard and after a free and informal discussion of the Standard, he should

ORGANIZATION CHART—Four Groups for About 21 to 25 Members and Prospects

Program Dates	Program Committee	Membership Committee	Missionary Committee	Bible Reading Committee	Social Committee
I.	Group Captain				
	President	Vice-President			
II.	Group Captain		Missionary Leader		
	Song Leader				
III.	Group Captain			Bible Readers' Leader	
	Pianist				
IV.	Group Captain				Social Leader
	Counselor	Secretary (Not on Comm.)			

Three Groups for About 18 to 20 Members and Prospects

Program Dates	Program Committee	Membership Committee	Missionary Committee	Bible Reading Committee	Social Committee
I.	Group Captain President	Vice-President			Social Leader
II.	Group Captain Counselor	Secretary (Not on Comm.)	Missionary Leader		
III.	Group Captain Pianist Song Leader			Bible Readers' Leader	

Two Groups for 12 Members or Less to About 17 Members and Prospects

Program Dates	Program Committee	Membership Committee	Missionary Committee	Bible Reading Committee	Social Committee
I.	Group Captain President Song Leader	Vice-President		Bible Readers' Leader	Social Leader
II.	Group Captain Pianist Counselor	Secretary (Not on Comm.)	Missionary Leader		

call upon the union to give a standing vote in favor of following the Standard and meeting the requirements.

6. *All Working Together*

The Standard of Excellence should be displayed before the union. Each point should be gone over carefully and seals should be placed upon all requirements already met by the union. Then each officer should stand before the union and agree that he will be responsible for his part in making the union Standard.

7. *The Secretary's Work*

While there is no requirement in the Standard of Excellence as to how the records should be kept, the manner in which the secretary keeps the records and makes reports will have an important bearing upon the progress the union makes in reaching the Standard. The secretary should keep the records of the union accurately and be able at all times to acquaint each officer with the status of every phase of the work relating to the Standard of Excellence. This should show in the weekly report of the

---

M
Y
P
L
E
D
G
E

Relying upon divine help, I purpose to be true to Christ in all things and at all times; to seek the New Testament standard of Christian experience and life; to be faithful in attending the meetings of my union; and to participate worthily in its activities, striving to "grow in grace, and in the knowledge of our Lord and Saviour Jesus Christ."

Signed _____

Address _____

Union _____ Date _____

TO MY UNION

FORM TU 1450, BROADMAN SUPPLIES, NASHVILLE, TENNESSEE. COPYRIGHT, 1951

secretary, and also in the secretary's report to the monthly officers' council.

The Standard of Excellence requires that at least two-thirds of the members, based on average enrolment for the quarter, make individual average grades for the quarter of at least 70 per cent on the Eight Point Record System. To figure the grade for each member, add his weekly grades for the quarter and divide by the number of Sundays in the quarter.

OUTLINE

I. FOLLOW THE STANDARD OF EXCELLENCE—THE TRAINING GUIDE OF THE BAPTIST YOUNG PEOPLE'S UNION

II. HOW TO ORGANIZE THE BAPTIST YOUNG PEOPLE'S UNION

1. Officers
2. Committees
3. Groups

III. HOW TO USE THE STANDARD OF EXCELLENCE AS THE TRAINING GUIDE

1. A Called Meeting of Officers
2. The Standard of Excellence Explained
3. Each Officer Should Assume Responsibility for His Part
4. Agree upon a Time Limit
5. The Union Should Vote to Reach the Standard
6. All Working Together
7. The Secretary's Work

CHAPTER *3*

The Young People's Department of the Baptist Training Union

THE ALERT, modern Training Union is departmentized in all churches which need the department organization. Every church should make a thorough appraisal of its total possibilities to determine the steps that are needed to set up an efficient, functioning department organization for the young people in the Training Union.

I. CHURCHES WHICH NEED YOUNG PEOPLE'S DEPARTMENT ORGANIZATION

1. *Where One Department Is Needed*

In churches having possibilities for two or more Young People's unions, ages 17–24, a department organization should be set up by the church to lead, supervise, and develop the young people's work. The ideal enrolment for one Young People's union ranges from about twenty to twenty-five. Of course, a union with much smaller enrolment can do splendid work. In many small churches it is often advisable to have at least two unions for young people in order to grade them into congenial groups. This would make it possible to have a union for the young people who range in age from seventeen to twenty, and another union for those twenty-one to twenty-four.

2. *Where Two Departments Are Needed*

All churches which have possibilities for two or more Young People's unions in the general age group seventeen to twenty, and possibilities for two or more unions in the age group twenty-one to twenty-four, should have at least two Young People's departments. These departments would be designated as Young People's department number one and Young People's department number two. In most cases, the complete department organization, as set out in this chapter, should be set up.

The same principles of grading apply where more than two departments are needed. The department divisions are made on an age basis except where a separate department is provided for married young people.

II. Purpose of the Young People's Department

The purpose of the department organization for young people is to set up and help build as many strong unions as are needed to reach and train in church membership all the young people of the church. The keynote of the Training Union is "Developing the Individual" through training in public testimony, prayer, giving, leadership in practical affairs, worship, and instruction in doctrine and missions. This training work, of course, is done in the individual unions. The department organization places definite responsibility upon department leadership for organizing and maintaining all the unions that are needed.

III. Standard of Excellence—The Training Guide for the Young People's Department

I. ORGANIZATION

1. *Officers.*—Director, associate director, secretary, song leader, and pianist, elected by the church. The director, associate director, and secretary shall hold, or earn during the quarter, an award on the Baptist Young People's Union Administration.

2. *Committee.*—Executive, composed of department officers, counselors, and presidents of unions.

3. *Grading.*—Two or more Young People's unions, graded by congenial age groups.

4. *Enrolment.*—One-half of the resident church membership, ages 17–24, shall be enrolled in the Young People's de-

partment of the Training Union. In churches with more than one Young People's department, each department shall meet this requirement for its age group.

II. MEETINGS

1. *Weekly Meetings.*—(1) The department shall conduct a weekly assembly of all unions, preferably before the union meetings. (2) The department shall co-operate with the Training Union in attendance upon any general assemblies which it may hold.

2. *Executive Committee Meeting.*—The department director shall hold a monthly meeting of the department officers, counselors, and presidents of unions to plan the work of the department for the coming month.

3. *Training Union Officers' Council.*—The department shall co-operate with the Training Union in its plan for the officers' council.

III. ACTIVITIES

1. *Study.*—(1) *Lesson Course.*—The Young People's department shall follow the lesson course in *Baptist Young People* or *Baptist Married Young People,* published by the Baptist Sunday School Board. (2) *Textbook Study Course.*—The Young People's department, in co-operation with the Training Union, shall conduct a study course for the unions at least once every twelve months, using the Young People's books of the Graded Training Union Study Course of the Baptist Sunday School Board.

2. *Daily Bible Reading.*—The Young People's department shall follow the Daily Bible Readers' Course for individual reading and daily devotions as published in *Baptist Young People* or *Baptist Married Young People.*

3. *Worship.*—(1) The Young People's department shall promote attendance upon the evening preaching service. (2) The Young People's department shall promote attendance upon the church prayer meeting.

4. *Stewardship and Missions.*—(1) The Young People's department shall promote education in stewardship, tithing, and the enlistment of all its members in systematic giving to church expenses, benevolences, and missions, according to the church plan. (2) The Young People's department shall encourage the enlistment of all its members in active service in other church activities and organizations. (3) The Young

People's department shall participate at least once each quarter in some practical missionary activity. (4) The Young People's department shall seek to enlist all its active members in praying for and witnessing to lost people daily.

5. *Social Life.*—The Young People's department shall promote a program of Christian social life as required in the Standard of the Young People's union. Once each year the unions may combine their socials into a department social.

6. *Visitation.*—Regular visitation of all absentees and prospects shall be sponsored.

IV. ACHIEVEMENT

At least one-half the unions of the Young People's department shall qualify as Standard unions for the quarter.

NOTE.—If the department has reached the points on this Standard for a quarter, application for the Standard award should be made in duplicate to the state Training Union secretary on forms furnished by him. To the department qualifying as Standard, the quarterly Standard award will be sent by the Baptist Sunday School Board.

Each department should send the names and addresses of its director, presidents, and counselors to the state Training Union department after each election of officers.

IV. DEPARTMENT OFFICERS

Upon recommendation of the Training Union director, the following department officers for the Young People's department should be elected by the church: department director, associate department director, department secretary, department song leader, and department pianist.

All department officers should be members of a Baptist church.

A brief discussion of the work of the department officers is given here.

1. *Department Director*

The department director may be a man or a woman. He should be a consecrated leader who is loyal to his church, and who is able to elicit the support and co-operation of the church for his department.

In order that he may be prepared for the work, the

department director should master each issue of *Baptist Young People* or *Baptist Married Young People,* BAPTIST YOUNG PEOPLE'S UNION ADMINISTRATION, *The Baptist Training Union Magazine,* and *The Baptist Training Union Manual.*

In the formulation of all plans and policies, the department director should consult the Training Union director and follow his leadership.

The department director will work along these lines:

(1) *Helping to find good counselors and presidents for the unions.*—It is very important to have leading men and women of the church as counselors of the Young People's unions and outstanding young people as presidents. In making plans for a new union, the department director should first find a man or woman to serve as counselor, and then help him to enlist a president and other members and complete the organization.

(2) *Organizing new unions.*—The department director should lead in organizing as many unions as are needed to reach and train all the church members between the ages of seventeen and twenty-four.

Young People's unions should be graded on the basis of congeniality within the prescribed age limits. The ideal number for the membership of a Young People's union ranges from twenty to twenty-five, but first-class work may be done by unions much smaller in size.

(3) *Leading the leaders.*—In co-operation with the general director, the department director is the leader of the leaders in his department. There are two classes of these:

a. Department officers.—The department director will lead the other department officers to do their work as outlined in this chapter.

b. Presidents and counselors of the unions.—The department director will accomplish his work largely through his leadership of those who have charge of the unions. He will lead them to accomplish the tasks as outlined below.

(*a*) *Enlistment.*—The president and counselor of each union must be led to carry on a continuous program of enlistment, aggressively seeking for membership in the union all those who have been assigned to them by the associate director of the Training Union.

(*b*) *Standardization.*—The Standard of Excellence for each union is the working program of that union. The department director should lead the president and counselor of each union to follow that program.

(*c*) *Improvement of the weekly meetings.*—The department director will visit the various unions from time to time and study their programs. He will then be in position to advise with the presidents and counselors concerning program building, preparation, and presentation. He should strive to lead each one to make a success of each weekly meeting.

(*d*) *Co-operation with the Training Union.*—The department director should lead each union of his department to co-operate in all the work of the Training Union. This involves the following:

Weekly assembly and preaching service.—Each union must be led to come into the general assembly and preaching service following the weekly meetings.

Executive committee meeting of Training Union.—The executive committee of the Training Union meets monthly usually one hour before Training Union time on the Sunday preceding the monthly officers' council. The department director should see that his department officers and the presidents and counselors of his unions are present. See page 49 for discussion of department executive committee meeting.

General monthly officers' council.—All general and department officers, all of the officers of unions above the Junior department, and the adult workers of the Junior, Primary, Beginner, and Nursery departments, should attend the general monthly officers' council. See page 50 for further discussion.

Training schools.—When the Training Union conducts

a training school, the department director should lead all his unions to co-operate.

Socials.—The department director will assist the unions in the matter of planning their own socials, so as to prevent conflicts and overlapping, and insure effectiveness.

Outside activities.—The department director will lead his unions to co-operate in all the plans of the Training Union for social service and Training Union extension work, and in co-operating with all other church work not directly connected with the Training Union.

(4) *Planning and conducting department assemblies.* —See pages 47 to 49 for discussion of this point.

(5) *Reporting to the Training Union.*—The department director should make a monthly written report to the Training Union at the executive committee meeting showing the number of unions, enrolment, new members, average attendance, Standard unions, Bible readers, givers, preaching attendance, grade of each union and department, and any other noteworthy work and plans for next month.

2. Associate Department Director

An associate department director should help the department director in all his work, but should have certain well-defined duties, as outlined here.

(1) *Assist the director in making his plans*

(2) *Preside at department meetings when called upon*

(3) *Help organize the unions*

(4) *Lead the vice-presidents of the unions in the following activities*: winning new members, visitation of absentees every week, promoting preaching and prayer meeting attendance, and encouraging all members to be on time in the weekly meeting. In all this work the associate department director will work with the associate director and membership committee of the Training Union.

(5) *Lead the missionary leaders of the unions in doing extension work*

MONTHLY REPORT OF DEPARTMENT DIRECTOR
OF THE.........................DEPARTMENT

TO BAPTIST TRAINING UNION
MONTHLY EXECUTIVE COMMITTEE MEETING

For ...., 19....

Number unions in department..

Enrolment: Active............ Associate .... Total ....

New members during month..

How many prospects are listed? ....

How many unions are Standard? ....Was department
Standard? ....

Number members making grade of 70% or above for the month ....
....

Was department executive committee meeting held?..................

Number present in officers' council (only adult workers required for
Juniors) ....

How many program committee meetings held? ....

Plans for next month...
....
...., Department Director
.... Department

Suggested Report Form

3. *Department Secretary*

The department secretary is in charge of records for the department. He should master thoroughly the Eight Point Record System and its use in the Training Union. His duties are as follows:

(1) *Train the secretaries of the unions.*—The department secretary, with the secretaries of the unions, should attend the monthly meeting of the efficiency committee of the Training Union, at the general monthly officers' council (or at the call of the general secretary), and there with the general secretary study how to make reports and keep records. He should also see that the secretaries of the unions attend this meeting.

(2) *See that the secretaries of the unions keep correct*

records and make reports.—The department secretary should examine the records of the union secretaries at least once a month and see that they are correct. He should also see that the secretary of each union makes the reports as indicated on page 97 and in chapter 6 of this book.

(3) *Get a weekly report from each union.*—The secretary of each union should make a weekly report to the department secretary, on the form below.

UNION SECRETARY'S WEEKLY REPORT

Sunday _____ 19____ Signed _____ Secretary

_____ Union	Enrolled	Absent	Present 10%	On Time 10%	Studied Lesson 15%	On Program 15%	Study Course 10%	Daily Bible Readers 15%	Attending Preaching 10%	Giving to Church 15%	Grade	No. Making 70% or Above
Group 1												
Group 2												
Group 3												
Group 4												
Totals Today												

	HOW TO FIGURE THE UNION GRADE	CONTACTS MADE
New Members	Multiply the number qualifying on each point by the value of that point, add the eight products thus obtained, and divide the sum by the total enrolment.	Visits ....
Visitors		Phone Calls....
Grand Total Present Today		Letters or cards____
Grand Total Present Last Sunday		Total ....
Totals Last Sunday		

FORM TU-1148 EIGHT POINT RECORD SYSTEM, BAPTIST SUNDAY SCHOOL BOARD NASHVILLE, TENN., COPYRIGHT, 1951, 2898

---

(4) *Make a weekly report to general secretary.*—The department secretary will transfer the totals from the union secretaries' reports to the card as indicated below, and send this report to the general secretary.

The department secretary should file a duplicate of the above for reference.

(5) *See that the president of each union makes a quarterly check on the Standard.*—The department secretary should see that the president of each union makes a complete check to determine whether the union has maintained Standard rating for the quarter. If the union is Standard, application for the Standard award should be made in duplicate to the state Training Union secretary.

DEPARTMENT SECRETARY'S WEEKLY REPORT
JUNIOR THROUGH ADULT
For department secretary's report to general secretary
For 6 unions or less

Sunday_____   19____ Signed _____Secretary

Dept. Unions	Enrolled	Absent	Present 10%	On Time 10%	Studied Lesson 15%	On Program 15%	Study Course 10%	Daily Bible Readers 15%	Attending Preaching 10%	Giving to Church 1%	New Members	Visitors	Total Present	Total Contacts	Grade	No. Making 70% or Above
Department Officers																
Totals Today																
Totals Last Sunday																

HOW TO FIGURE THE DEPARTMENT GRADE

Multiply the number qualifying on each point by the value of that point, add the eight products thus obtained, and divide the sum by the total enrolment.

FORM TU-1225 EIGHT POINT RECORD SYSTEM, BAPTIST SUNDAY SCHOOL BOARD, NASHVILLE, TENN., COPYRIGHT, 1951, BSSB

Form TU-1230 is a double card with spaces for as many
as twenty unions in one department.

Application blanks may be secured from the state Training Union office or from the Training Union Department,
Baptist Sunday School Board, Nashville 3, Tennessee.

4. *Department Song Leader*

The department song leader should retain membership
and work in a union. His duties are to help plan and lead
the singing for department assemblies or other department meetings which may be held. See chapter 7.

5. *Department Pianist*

What has been said above with reference to the person
serving as song leader is also true concerning the pianist.
The pianist should help plan all department music and
play for all department singing. See chapter 7.

V. DEPARTMENT MEETINGS

1. *Department Assembly*

An opening assembly of all unions should be held every

Sunday by the Young People's department, with the department director in charge.

The department assembly gives the department director an opportunity to lead his department in a constructive program of work, creates unity in the department and generates spirit and enthusiasm for the work.

The department director is directly responsible for the department assembly programs. Any plans involving the participation of the unions should be discussed in the executive committee meetings of the department, in which the department officers, counselors, and presidents meet with the department director to make plans and to determine policies for the department organization.

The opening assembly program should usually consist of the following:

Quiet music as members assemble

Song

Prayer

Brief Scripture reading

Special feature

Announcements

Adjourn to various meeting places

Suggestions for the department assembly programs may be found in the Young People's section of *The Baptist Training Union Magazine*. The department director should regularly use the young people in presenting these programs. They should literally be programs *by* young people. However, the department director should keep in mind that these programs must be brief, for the primary work of training comes in the individual unions, following the opening assembly. Usually the time allotted to the opening assembly is fifteen minutes. At least forty-five minutes, and preferably fifty-five minutes, should be allotted to the union meetings. Most departmentized Training Unions do not have a general assembly of all the unions except as a part of the evening preaching service. This is known as the integrated service.

The time schedule for the whole period would then be as follows:

6:15 Opening department assembly
6:30 Union meetings
7:25 Adjourn to church auditorium
7:30 Evening preaching service with brief Training Union feature during announcement period

2. *Executive Committee Meeting*

The department executive committee, composed of department officers and counselors and presidents of the unions, should meet about a week before the general monthly officers' council every month. It should meet as a part of the Training Union executive committee. The opening period of the general monthly executive committee meeting of the Training Union is devoted to the departments. In the second period all come together for the general executive committee meeting.

The department director is required to make a written report on the work of his department to the Training Union executive committee meeting. The form for this is suggested in the discussion of the work of the department director in this chapter.

In the department executive committee meeting, full instructions are given to the counselors and presidents of the unions concerning their preparation for the monthly officers' council and the plans they should make for their unions for the coming month. Each president should be given copies of the monthly review and plan sheet for all the officers of his union, with the request that these be filled out and presented to the monthly officers' council. Copies of these suggested forms are given in the various chapters of this manual.

Programs for the department assemblies should be planned here also. Use suggestions in the Young People's department of *The Baptist Training Union Magazine.*

All problems, plans, and policies for the Young People's

department should be discussed in the executive committee meeting.

3. *Training Union Officers' Council*

All department officers and the officers of all unions in the Young People's department should attend the monthly Training Union officers' council. The president of each union will have opportunity there to meet with the officers of his union and plan the work of the union for the coming month. Provision is made at the general officers' council for the program committees of the various unions to meet in a pre-session meeting.

The presidents of the unions should make written reports to the department director at the council. See page 66 for form.

VI. DEPARTMENT ACTIVITIES

The department director should lead all the unions to follow faithfully the lesson courses in *Baptist Young People* or *Baptist Married Young People,* published by the Baptist Sunday School Board. As indicated above, he should arrange for all program committees of all unions to meet in connection with the general monthly officers' council to plan the programs for the following month.

The department director should assume responsibility, in co-operation with the Training Union director, for planning at least one training school for taking study courses each year. He will lead the presidents and group captains of the unions in the enlistment of all the members to take the study course.

Another fruitful activity for the department director is the leadership of all the unions in the matter of the enlistment of all members in daily Bible reading and daily prayer.

The associate director of the department, working with the vice-presidents of the union, should seek to lead all the young people to attend the evening worship services of the church and also the midweek prayer meeting.

For education in stewardship and missions, the department officers should lead all the unions to study faithfully the regular lessons in *Baptist Young People* or *Baptist Married Young People,* to take the textbook study courses on stewardship and missions, and do everything in their power to encourage all the members of the department to participate in active service in all other church activities and organizations, such as the Sunday school.

In addition to the foregoing, the Young People's department officers should seek to lead all the unions to participate in outside missionary activities, such as extension work of the Training Union in other churches; and work in Negro churches to organize unions, teach study courses, and help with their meetings.

The climax of all missionary service is personal soul-winning. There should be perennial emphasis in the department on personal witnessing to the lost. The missionary committees should be encouraged to lead all the members of all the unions to participate in this highest of all Christian service.

The department director should seek to lead all unions to promote a constructive program of Christian social life as required in the Standards of the unions. As indicated in the Standard, once each year the unions may combine their socials into a department social. It is well to remember in this connection that a union may combine with other church organizations, such as Sunday school classes, at least twice each year in holding socials.

The associate director and vice-presidents of the unions promote the program of visitation for the department. The only way to build a great Young People's department is through continuous and persistent visitation.

The associate director and vice-presidents should meet each month with the general membership committee of which the associate director of the Training Union is chairman. This meets in the first period of the general monthly officers' council.

VII. DEPARTMENT ACHIEVEMENT

The department officers should seek to lead each union to set up the Standard of Excellence as its training guide and to strive each quarter to fulfil all the requirements of this guide. Any Young People's union which works faithfully at the job can become a Standard union.

It should be kept in mind at all times that the practical activities outlined for the department and the unions are not ends within themselves but are means to a lofty end, namely, spiritual efficiency in the service of Christ.

SUGGESTIONS FOR FURTHER STUDY AND DISCUSSION

1. Make a survey of the membership of your church showing the following:
   (1) Approximately how many members are there between the ages of seventeen and twenty?
   (2) Approximately how many members are there between the ages of twenty-one and twenty-four?
2. In what way do you think the Young People's department organization would help to build a greater training program for young people in your church?
3. If you do not have a Young People's department organization, request the Training Union director to work with you during this study to find a department director and set up a complete department organization.

OUTLINE

I. CHURCHES WHICH NEED YOUNG PEOPLE'S DEPARTMENT ORGANIZATION
   1. Where One Department Is Needed
   2. Where Two Departments Are Needed

II. PURPOSE OF THE YOUNG PEOPLE'S DEPARTMENT

III. STANDARD OF EXCELLENCE—THE TRAINING GUIDE FOR THE YOUNG PEOPLE'S DEPARTMENT

IV. DEPARTMENT OFFICERS

1. Department Director
2. Associate Department Director
3. Department Secretary
4. Department Song Leader
5. Department Pianist

V. DEPARTMENT MEETINGS

1. Department Assembly
2. Executive Committee Meeting
3. Training Union Officers' Council

VI. DEPARTMENT ACTIVITIES

VII. DEPARTMENT ACHIEVEMENT

CHAPTER 4

The President, Counselor, and Group Captain

I. THE PRESIDENT

The president is elected and placed in charge of the Young People's union to make it succeed. The success of the union depends upon his leadership. If he fails, the union fails. If the union succeeds, it is because of his intelligent and aggressive leadership. If he is not willing to assume responsibility for the success of the union in the fullest measure, and will not agree to put the necessary time, study, and work into it to make it succeed, he ought not to accept the office.

The president is elected, not to boss the union, not even to manage it, but to lead it intelligently and vigorously, to secure the co-operation of the officers and committees, and to train and develop all the members individually.

1. *The President's Personal Qualifications*

(1) *Spiritual fitness.*—The president's task is a spiritual task, pre-eminently, dealing with the spiritual development of the young people. In order to lead in their spiritual development he must have a spiritual equipment for his work. The spiritual side of his own life must have constant attention. He should have a keen appreciation of spiritual values, keeping the spiritual aim uppermost in all his thinking and planning. He should utilize every means at hand for the cultivation and enrichment of his personal life, spiritually, at the same time striving for the highest spiritual development of the young people.

a. The president will keep fit spiritually by cultivating

54

his prayer life.—Prayer must have a place in his life daily. The habit of prayer must dominate his life. Unless he prays, he cannot lead the union to a high state of spiritual attainment. It should be his aim to lead every member of the union to covenant with him to engage daily in secret prayer. Thus in communion with Christ will the president and the young people grow strong spiritually and become more like Christ day by day. The president should also train all the members of the union to lead in public prayer which will serve as a means of further developing them spiritually. In order to do this effectually the president must attend carefully to his own prayer life.

b. The president will grow strong spiritually through studying his Bible daily.—By daily Bible study the president will get in close personal touch with God. He will thus be able to know and appropriate the promises of God. Let the president make God's Word the "man of his counsel"; let him read it, and love it. The shameful, sinful neglect of the Bible on the part of God's children, both old and young, is appalling. Let the president study his Bible daily and let him call the young people back to the Word of God. In so doing he will "grow in grace, and in the knowledge of our Lord and Saviour Jesus Christ," and also make the greatest possible contribution toward the spiritual development of the young people. The president should so study and know his Bible that he can in his deepest soul say with the psalmist, "The law of thy mouth is better unto me than thousands of gold and silver" (Psalm 119:72).

c. The president will make spiritual advancement as he gives himself industriously to his work.—He must actually *work*. Close attention to his work will fit the president spiritually for his tasks. He will suffer spiritual decline every time he neglects his work. As he faithfully and vigorously leads the young people in all the activities of the union, his spiritual strength will be renewed. Working for Christ at Christ's tasks is as sure a means of spiritual growth as prayer and Bible study. The three supplement one another. All are necessary. The neglect of one means the weakening of all, and spiritual decline is sure to follow speedily.

Any task or service for Christ well done means the accumulation of spiritual strength for other tasks. Working for Christ means growing in Christ. Doing "with our might" for Christ the tasks assigned us in the Young People's union means spiritual energy stored up for yet greater tasks.

As the president faithfully performs his duties as the leader of the union, he will have added strength for the problems that come with each new task.

(2) *Other qualities of leadership.*—Let us consider some of the essential characteristics of a successful Young People's union president.

a. Enthusiasm.—Enthusiasm is a rare and charming quality and is an essential in successful leadership in any undertaking. It is inherent in some people and may be acquired in a degree at least by all. It marks the difference between a successful leader and a failure anywhere and everywhere. Enthusiasm takes account of difficulties only to overcome them.

An enthusiastic president will readily impart his spirit to the entire union and in so doing he will find the young people easily responsive to his leadership.

If at any time the president should find his enthusiasm for the Young People's union work on the wane, let him earnestly make a re-study of the work and redouble his efforts to make the union succeed, and he will find the tide of his enthusiasm rapidly rising, and joy and blessing will be his as a result.

b. Energy.—Someone has truly said that "the difference between one man and another is not mere ability; it is energy." The man who walks in his sleep is not to be feared, but the man "who sleeps in his walk" causes trouble everywhere. Energetic people are doing Christ's service. Lazy people are not more successful in Christ's service than elsewhere; they are failures wherever they are found.

A lazy person is as certain to fail as president of the Young People's union as the sun is to shine. Lazy people do not lead; they are always behind. Like Lot's wife, they start late and stay behind all the time.

The Young People's union president in his work with the young people is dealing with life at full tide. He is called upon to lead the energetic, ambitious, restless, growing young people, and he will find that ceaseless, tireless work will be necessary to do this effectively. Every faculty and member—heart, mind, hands, and feet—must be put into active operation for Christ. Satisfaction and joy, which are the accompanists of success, come only to the president who is indeed "a doer of the word."

c. Initiative.—The Young People's union president must have the ability to originate; to improvise; to adapt new methods in such an intelligent and attractive manner that the young people will gladly adopt them and co-operate with him in making them effective. The president must be able to "start something"; also to take a suggested method and improve it as he works it out in his union.

How one suffers in spirit as he hears presidents here and there say of approved Young People's union plans and methods, "Those methods won't work here." "We tried that and it failed." "The group plan won't work in our union." "Our young people just won't read their Bibles." "Our young people won't take part on the program." In most such cases the trouble is with the president. He does not master his work. He does not know how. He does not make a beginning. He doesn't go anywhere. He is a young fossil. Let the president get an intelligent conception of his work; let him welcome suggestions; let him take hold with both hands; let him introduce new methods into the union and he will find the young people ready and anxious to co-operate.

2. *The President's Preparation for His Work*

The president will not be able to "just naturally" make the union go. He will have to study all phases of Young

People's union work and keep studying the work all the time. He will also be compelled to make a close and constant study of the young people themselves in order to use and develop them. Let us take these points up in order and see how this may be done.

(1) *The president studying the work.*—The president should begin his work by mastering the Standard of Excellence. It presents the plans for organization, meetings, and activities of the union. Following this he should master this book, and study regularly the quarterly and *The Baptist Training Union Magazine*. He should also procure all the free literature on the Young People's union and master it. He must be able to instruct all officers and committees in their duties.

(2) *The president studying the workers.*—The president's ability to direct wisely the activities of the Young People's union will be gauged in a large measure by his personal knowledge of the members. This knowledge will assist him in keeping a good organization and in helping the members in their Christian growth.

There will be opportunity for the president to study the members outside the union: at school, at their daily occupations, through personal contact in a social way, through the records of the union, and by observing them in the other services of the church.

He will have other opportunities to observe the members of the union in the meetings. He should note the way they participate in the weekly meetings, at the officers' council, during union socials, and during training schools or study courses.

Making proper use of these contacts will help the president lead intelligently in the work of the Young People's union.

3. *The President and the Weekly Meetings*

One important task of every president is to see that a successful meeting is conducted each week. The president will want to keep in mind that, to a large extent, the degree to which a union is succeeding can be measured by what takes place on Sunday evening at the weekly meeting. This is true because the weekly meeting reflects the work done in the program planning meeting and at the officers' council. It also reveals the work done by the members, officers, and committees during the week. This, then, is the climax experience of the week and is worthy of all the intelligent thought, planning, and preparation which the president can put into it. Much of the success of the Sunday evening meeting depends on what is done before Sunday.

The president should be on hand fully twenty minutes before the weekly meeting is scheduled to begin. This time can be well spent making certain everything is in readiness. The president can meet the young people, and confer with officers about plans for the evening.

As the presiding officer of the union, the president should constantly strive to improve himself. He should remember that the manner and attitude he assumes in presiding over the meetings is reflected in the attitude of the members toward the union itself. He should see that the meetings begin, run, and close on time. He should be cheerful, tactful, and optimistic before the union. He should publicly give praise when it is due, but he should give words of advice or criticism privately.

The president should have a written schedule for each meeting of the union. The schedule suggested here may be used as a pattern for the weekly meeting.

A SUGGESTED YOUNG PEOPLE'S UNION SCHEDULE

I. Department Assembly (15 minutes)

   (If there is no department assembly, or general opening assembly, there should be a devotional period in the union. The devotional period usually consists of music, Scripture reading and prayer, and sometimes a special feature.)

II. Union Meeting (55 minutes)—President presiding
  1. Prayer
  2. Opening period (10 minutes):
     Secure records
     Make announcements
     Have committee reports:
       Program—Group captain in charge of next Sunday's program gives brief preview and/or assigns discussions.
       Social—Brief report, recognizes visitors
       Membership—Brief report; presents new members

       Missionary—Brief report
       Bible reading—Brief report ⎱ These two committees may prefer to report in connection with their features suggested in points 3 and 4 below.
  3. Bible drill (6 minutes)—Bible readers' leader
  4. Missionary feature (3 minutes)—Missionary leader
  5. Secretary's report (1 minute)
  6. Program period (30 minutes)—Group captain
     (A period of open discussion should frequently come at the close of the program period.)
  7. Prayer for evening preaching service

4. *The President and the Weekly Meeting Programs*

The president is responsible for having all the work of the union done. He cannot do everything himself, and should not, even if he were able. He must do his work through others. While not directly charged with building the programs, at the same time he is responsible for the success of each of the programs, and must see that they are properly planned and well executed. Let us see what he should do to insure their success.

(1) *Planning the programs.*—The president should call a monthly program planning meeting to plan all the programs for the succeeding month. All of the members of the program committee should be present at this meeting: president, group captains, and counselor. The Bible read-

ers' leader, the missionary leader, and the social leader should also meet with this committee.

The program committee meeting should be held prior to the officers' council so that these officers will be prepared to tell of their plans for the coming month at the council meeting. It is usually held on the same evening thirty or forty-five minutes before the officers' council.

The president should designate the topics assigned to each group at least a week before the program planning meeting. The group captains can then study their programs and make preliminary plans before coming to the meeting.

The president and group captains should see that all necessary materials for planning the programs are brought to the meeting: Bibles, copies of *Baptist Young People* or *Baptist Married Young People,* books and magazines giving supplementary materials. Every member of the program committee should have a copy of *The Baptist Training Union Magazine* so that he can use the suggestions for program building found in the Young People's section as well as the supplementary program material found in the feature articles each month.

Care should be given in the meeting to assigning parts on the program. Every member of the union should be assigned discussions, each taking part when his group has charge.

(2) *Printing the programs.*—If possible, an outline of the programs for each month should be duplicated in a small folder for distribution to all members of the union. This helps to avoid misunderstanding regarding the parts assigned.

If it is impractical to make these folders each month, it is always advisable to make a typed outline of the program for the bulletin board or to give each member a typed outline of the programs in which he is to participate. The following footnote at the bottom of each program would be helpful: "Each member is expected to prepare his part on this program and not read from the quarterly." Reading from the quarterly cannot be counted on the Standard or the Eight Point Record System.

(3) *Assigning the programs.*—If the program committee expects the young people to take part, it is of the greatest importance that each member shall be definitely and intelligently assigned his part on the program. Often group captains fail to do this and wonder why the young people read out of the quarterly, or stay away from the meeting when put on the program.

In assigning parts on the program, written notice should be given and the necessary materials for preparing each part should be furnished each one on the program.

Lax, tardy, and slipshod methods in assigning the programs are responsible in the majority of cases for the failure of the young people to do a creditable job with their assignments. Parts on the program should always be given out a full week in advance. The president should provide a time in the weekly meeting for this to be done.

5. *The President and the Study Course*

The president, in co-operation with the group captains, should see that each member of the union completes at least one study course each year. In order to accomplish this, he must have an intelligent understanding of the purpose and plan of the Baptist Young People's Union Study Course.

(1) *Purpose of the study course*

a. To train the young people in effective Young People's union methods

b. To build up the young people spiritually

c. To teach and train the young people in missions

d. To teach Baptist young people what it means to be a Baptist

e. To teach and train the young members of Baptist churches how to be useful church members

f. To inspire our Baptist young people with denominational loyalty

g. To provide a broader background for the training experiences of the Young People's union

(2) *Study course textbooks.*—The purpose of the study course, as outlined above, is admirably met in the study course textbooks published by the Baptist Sunday School Board. These books cover a wide range of subjects. The diploma is shown here.

A complete list of the books under each subject of the study course may be secured by requesting the tract, "The Graded Training Union Study Course for all Church Members," from your state Training Union secretary or from the Training Union Department, Baptist Sunday School Board, Nashville 3, Tennessee.

(3) *Encouraging Study Course Work*

a. In regular study courses.—The president will want to work with the department director and the Training Union director in planning study course work. A study course for a Young People's union is usually held in connection with the graded church study courses rather than at a special time. A graded course should be offered twice each year. The president should advise with his Training Union leaders in selecting a suitable time and a competent teacher for each course.

Study course textbooks need to be provided at least a

week in advance of the study course. This will give young people an opportunity to make proper preparation for class participation by reading the book in advance.

The president and group captains should personally invite and urge each member of the union to join the class and take the course. A close check should be kept on the attendance, and absentees should be followed up each day.

The requirements for study course work may be found at the end of this book.

b. In special study courses.—Sometimes young people will desire an additional study course to meet certain felt needs. For example, when a topic is introduced in a program of the Young People's union and the young people feel the need for additional information, a study course may be planned. On such occasions the schedule may be worked out to suit the convenience of the union membership.

In other instances, young people may like to have a week-end camp with the program built around a study course textbook. This is a wonderful opportunity to combine fellowship and study.

c. Through home study.—After a week of study the president and group captains should check to see what members of the union have not completed a study course during the past year and thus cannot count "study course" on the Eight Point Record System each week. For these members a home study course should be encouraged using one of the approved textbooks. Requirements for home study are given at the end of this book.

This plan of study can also be encouraged for alert members who desire extra study courses. In no instance, however, should home study courses take the place of classwork with a competent teacher.

d. By working toward a goal.—The president should keep before the union the idea of completing at least one book in each of the ten divisions of the Young People's union study course.

A diploma may be secured by completing the study of this book. A seal number 1 is awarded for taking this course the second time. Seals are awarded for completing each of the books in the other nine subjects of the study course. When a diploma is filled with seals the owner may apply for the Award of Merit.

After one course is completed in each of the ten subjects the president should encourage the young people to take other books, according to their interest and need, and place the seals on their diplomas.

6. *The President and the Records*

The president should keep a record of the work of each member of the union for his own guidance. He may secure this from the secretary's record. The president must know what each member of the union is doing, first, in order to co-operate intelligently with the officers in making their work effective; second, in order to assist the members in the solution of their individual problems. A Young People's union president's notebook may be secured from the Baptist Book Store serving your state.

7. *The President and the Monthly Officers' Council*

The president should hold a monthly council of all his officers to plan the work of the union for the next month. He should ask the group captains to come about thirty minutes earlier than the other officers to plan the programs. The Bible readers' leader, the missionary leader, and the social leader should meet with this committee.

In the officers' council all the work of the union is reviewed and plans made for the next month. Each officer, including the president, submits written plans.

The officers' council is a part of the monthly officers' council of the Training Union. When the union council is finished all the officers should assemble with the Training Union officers' council, where the president will make a written report for his union. In organized Young People's

---

PRESIDENT'S MONTHLY REVIEW AND PLAN SHEET

.... Union

SUBMITTED TO OFFICERS' COUNCIL

For Month of ...., 19....

1. Names of program committee members

    Group one ....

    Group two ....

    Group three ....

    Group four ....

2. Attended Training Union executive committee meeting (department executive committee if department is organized) ....

    Plans to report from executive committee ....

    ....

3. Program committee meeting held.................................

4. Plans for next month

    (1) Plans for weekly meetings

    Date_____ Subject_____ Leader _____

    Date_____ Subject_____ Leader _____

    Date_____ Subject_____ Leader _____

    Date_____ Subject_____ Leader _____

    Date_____ Subject_____ Leader _____

    (2) Other plans ....

    ....

    ....

    .... President

    .... Union

---

departments the president makes this report to the department director and he reports to the Training Union. A form for the president's report is suggested here.

II. THE ADULT COUNSELOR

Every Young People's union would be benefited by having an adult counselor. Sometimes a man and his wife may work together as joint counselors of a union.

The counselor should be elected by the church, upon the recommendation of the Training Union director, after he

---

MONTHLY REPORT OF PRESIDENT

of the.................................Union

TO DEPARTMENT EXECUTIVE COMMITTEE MEETING

(If you do not have a department make this report to the Training Union executive committee.)

For Month of ...., 19....

Did you attend monthly Training Union officers' council past month?...

....

Number present in officers' council past month ....

Program committee meeting held...

Are all programs planned for next month?...............................

Average enrolment for the past month....................................

Number new members during month.......................................

When was last social held?..

Grade of union for month...

Number of members making grade of 70% or above for past month

....

Is union Standard?...........................If not, name points lacking

....

....

Are officers and committees working?....................................

Special work done ....

Plans for next month..

....

...., President

.... Union

---

has advised with the department director and the president of the union.

The counselor, as the title indicates, counsels with the president and officers, and helps to guide the union in a constructive program of study and activity.

The counselor should study this book, *Baptist Young People* or *Baptist Married Young People, The Baptist Training Union Magazine,* and all available free literature on the Young People's union. He should master the Standard of Excellence, which is the training guide of the union.

The duties of the counselor may be defined as follows.

1. Lead the Union to Maintain a Functioning Organization of Officers, Committees, and Groups

2. Help the President to Instruct All Officers and Committees in Their Duties, as Required by the Standard of Excellence

3. Attend the Program Committee Meeting and Help Plan the Weekly Meeting Programs

4. Attend the Officers' Council and Advise with the Officers on All Plans and Policies

5. Attend Each Weekly Meeting

6. Guide the Union in Its Social Life and Attend Every Social

7. Guide the Union in All the Activities Outlined in the Standard, and Inspire It to Make a Quarterly Average Grade of at least 70 Per Cent

8. Help to Plan the Study Courses and Attend the Classes with the Young People

III. THE GROUP CAPTAIN

The group plan of organization is not an accident. It is a development in which many workers have had a part. So far as our information goes, the group plan was first employed as a means of getting the young people interested in the daily Bible readers' course in a very large union. All the members of the union were divided into four groups, with a captain in charge of each group, his main responsibility being to encourage and assist the young people in reading their Bibles daily.

The next step was easy, that of having the programs rendered by these different groups. Indeed, so effective a method in getting the young people to take part on the program was the "group plan" that soon it was realized, in order to get the best results, the Young People's union should be organized on the group basis for the accomplishment of all phases of Young People's union work.

It seems that the group plan came, in the providence of

God, to help our Baptist churches solve the difficult problem of reaching and developing, in an individual way, the great host of their young members. The group plan of organization seems divinely sent to help Baptist churches in realizing a cherished wish to develop and use in service for Christ all the church members.

The group plan of organization makes it possible for a church to single out each member of the union and give him individual attention, thus carrying out the motto, "All Baptist Young People Utilized."

Let us make a study of the work of the group captain and see how far-reaching his duties are in making practical and effective this motto.

1. Study the Members of His Group

Each group captain should make a careful study of each member of his group. A knowledge of what each one is capable of doing will necessarily form a true basis upon which he will be able to work with and develop them. In properly assisting the president in the formation of the different committees, this knowledge will be helpful. Also in assigning the different parts on the programs, this information will be practically indispensable.

The group captain should know of the aims and ambitions of all the young people in his group, and of what each one is capable of doing. He will thus be able to help and encourage them in every worthy effort.

He should know the special talents of each member in order to assist the president in utilizing them in service. Some are possessed with musical talents; some have gifts of social leadership; some are studiously inclined; some have teaching gifts; some are born leaders; some should become missionaries, perhaps; some should preach the gospel; some have an intensive soul-winning desire; and some are not Christians. The group captain should have all this information at hand in order to properly develop and utilize the young people to the best advantage.

2. Build Up the Group

(1) *New Members.*—The group captain should co-operate with the membership committee in seeking to enlist new members. Much of this work should be done by the member of his group who is on the membership committee. Some of the new members will be placed on his group. Thus the group captain can build up his group by co-operating with the membership committee.

(2) *Absentees.*—Likewise the group captains should co-operate with the membership committee in visiting each absentee of his group each week. At no time should he be willing to "drop" names from his group simply because the members are irregular in attendance. He should be so sympathetic and hopeful and helpful that the members will be constrained to become regular and attentive in their duties toward the union.

(3) *Provide a way for all to attend.*—Many people would join the union if a convenient way were afforded them to attend. The thoughtful group captain will give attention to this matter.

He should know fully twelve hours before the meeting what members in this group, if any, are not expecting to attend the union. Then, if possible, he should seek to overcome the difficulties in the way and have each member of his group present, and when the individual reports are made up he should be able to account for each member.

3. Member of Program Committee

The group captains are members of the program committee, and each group captain is responsible for the success of the program each time his group has charge.

The group captain should assume the leadership in planning the programs of the weekly meeting. He should always respond to the call of the president for the monthly meeting of the program committee and attend this meeting promptly. He should study his program carefully and make a preliminary outline of it before coming to this meeting.

He should have a complete roll of his group at the program committee meeting, and, in arranging the programs, he should see that every member of his group is put on the program.

He should assign the different parts on the program to each member of his group. This should be done one week ahead of time, at the weekly meeting.

He should also provide the necessary material to each member of his group to study his part and see that each one is prepared with his part when the time arrives for giving the program. The group captain should realize that he is the leader of his group and be willing to assume responsibility in every case of failure.

Periodically the group captain should ask a qualified member of his group to take charge of the program he has planned. When this is done the member who takes charge should know a week in advance. This will give additional training to the members of his group.

4. *Responsible for the Development of Each Member of His Group*

Growth and strength come through exercise, physically, mentally, and spiritually. In order to develop spiritually, the young people must take part on the programs, read the Bible, sing, pray, speak, and engage actively in every part of the work fostered in the union. All must do this. If left to themselves, only a few of the most capable, strongest, most forward young people will participate in the activities of the union. The backward and hesitant will only come and "sit and listen." This sort of process will not produce strong, vigorous soldiers of Christ. They must take part. They must stand on their feet and walk for Christ. The sitting position is a deadly posture for a Christian soldier.

It is the business of the group captain to develop all his

members by taking advantage of every opportunity afforded in the union to use them. Let us again call attention to these opportunities briefly and how each member may be developed.

(1) *In the weekly meeting.*—The group captain must find a way for a place on each program for using every member of his group. Each member should take part actively on the program. Some may read the Scripture lesson for the evening; others may memorize and quote verses of Scripture; others may give illustrations secured from the Bible or other sources; and others may discuss the topics as outlined in the quarterly. All should be led to pray in public.

A wise group captain will lead each member gradually from the most simple to the more difficult parts on the program.

(2) *Doing committee work.*—Every committee must have a representative from each one of the groups. This affords fine opportunity for training all the young people. The group captain should be able to suggest to the president and committee chairmen which members can serve best on the different committees, when they are formed. He should also co-operate with the committeemen in his group in doing their work. He should realize the value of doing committee work as a means of teaching the young people how to co-operate with their fellow members in securing desirable ends.

(3) *Taking the Bible readers' course.*—From his records the group captain will note whether or not every member of his group is keeping up with the daily Bible readers' course. In every case of failure to do so he should wisely and industriously set himself to the task of getting all such members to read their Bibles. Let the group captain know assuredly that he will fail in the highest development of the members of his group if they fail to read their Bibles. The spiritual growth and usefulness of all his members is absolutely dependent upon their reading their Bibles.

(4) *Taking the study course.*—The group captain should co-operate with the president in the enlistment of every member of his group in the annual or semiannual study course classes. Many of the young people will not join these classes unless urged to do so. Many others will join the classes and begin the work. The group captain should earnestly and patiently encourage them to go through with the classwork and take the examination. The study course work in the Young People's union has made a most wonderful contribution toward the development of our young people.

(5) *Studying the weekly programs.*—The group captain is responsible for enlisting the members of his group in studying every program in the quarterly, every week, regardless of when they are on the program.

5. *Keeps a Record of His Members*

The group captain should know what each member of his group is doing. This information he cannot have unless he keeps a record of the work of each. Therefore, there has been provided a group captain's record book in which the work of each member should be noted. It will be a simple matter for the group captain to secure from the secretary the individual reports of his members immediately following the meetings and transfer these reports to his record. This record book may be secured from the Baptist Book Store serving your area.

There is a large place of service for every officer in the Young People's union, and all may be busy about their tasks at all times. A president who is blessed with consecrated, intelligent, energetic, sympathetic group captains will find his task of developing the members of the Young People's union comparatively easy, so wide in scope and so fraught with possibilities are their duties.

6. *Attends the Monthly Officers' Council*

The group captain should attend the monthly officers' council of his union, where he will meet with the program committee in a pre-session meeting to plan the programs, and in the officers' council to help plan all the work of the union for the next month. In the officers' council the group captain will submit in writing his plans for the next month. A form for this is suggested herewith.

GROUP CAPTAIN'S MONTHLY REVIEW AND PLAN SHEET

.... Union

.... Group

SUBMITTED TO OFFICERS' COUNCIL

For Month of.., 19.....

1. Number enrolled in group first of past month........................

   Number enrolled now ....

2. Attended program committee meeting................................

3. Plans for next program

   (1) Date _____ Subject _____

   (2) Assignments to group members:

Subject	Name
Subject_____	Name_____
Subject_____	Name_____
Subject_____	Name_____
Subject_____	Name_____
Subject_____	Name_____

   (3) Special plans for weekly meeting..................................

   ....

   ....

4. Plans for other work...

   ....

   ....

   ....Group Captain

   ....Union

OUTLINE

I. THE PRESIDENT

1. The President's Personal Qualifications
2. The President's Preparation for his Work
3. The President and the Weekly Meetings
4. The President and the Weekly Meeting Programs
5. The President and the Study Course
6. The President and the Records
7. The President and the Monthly Officers' Council

II. THE ADULT COUNSELOR

1. Lead the Union to Maintain a Functioning Organization of Officers, Committees, and Groups
2. Help the President to Instruct All Officers and Committees in Their Duties, as Required by the Standard of Excellence
3. Attend the Program Committee Meeting and Help Plan the Weekly Meeting Programs
4. Attend the Officers' Council and Advise with the Officers on All Plans and Policies
5. Attend Each Weekly Meeting
6. Guide the Union in Its Social Life and Attend Every Social
7. Guide the Union in All the Activities Outlined in the Standard, and Inspire It to Make a Quarterly Average Grade of at Least 70 Per Cent
8. Help to Plan the Study Courses and Attend the Classes with the Young People

III. THE GROUP CAPTAIN

1. Study the Members of His Group
2. Build Up the Group
3. Member of Program Committee
4. Responsible for the Development of Each Member of His Group
5. Keeps a Record of His Members
6. Attends the Monthly Officers' Council

CHAPTER 5

The Vice-President and Missionary Leader

I. THE VICE-PRESIDENT

1. *Presides in the Absence of the President*

The vice-president should have some platform ability. He should at least be able to preside with ease and express himself with clearness. The ability to do this will come with experience and observation. A knowledge of the work generally and knowing what he is to do in particular will serve in giving him confidence in himself. He should be able to maintain order in the union and conduct the programs with intelligence and dispatch. Frequently the president should call upon the vice-president to preside, in this way giving him an opportunity for practice which is essential in his training.

2. *Chairman of the Membership Committee*

The vice-president should have more to do than simply to preside at the weekly meetings occasionally. Hence, he is made chairman of the membership committee, and the important work of building up the union is entrusted to his leadership.

(1) *The membership committee.*—This committee is composed of the vice-president as chairman and a member from each one of the groups. It is the specific duty of each member of this committee to work with the captain of his particular group, building up that group. At a glance it is easily seen that this method of locating the duties and work of committees does away with the usual

vagueness which maintains in connection with practically all committees. In this way each member of each committee works in his own group and need never be in doubt as to what he should do.

(2) *The Young People's union membership.*—As we have seen in another chapter the Young People's union membership is of two kinds—active and associate.

a. The active membership.—Those eligible for active membership in the Young People's union are Baptist church members, seventeen through twenty-four years of age.

b. The associate membership.—The associate membership is composed of young people in a community who are not Christians and also those of other denominations who may desire to join the union.

3. *Work of the Membership Committee*

The work of the membership committee in building up the union is twofold: That of reaching new members, and following up the absentees.

(1) *Reaching new members.*—In the average Baptist church there is a sufficient number of younger members for at least one Young People's union. In many churches there are enough young people for two and often a large number of Young People's unions. The following are the definite sources of information from which the membership committee may discover prospective members for the Young People's union.

a. Church roll
b. Sunday school roll
c. Religious census
d. Preaching service

The vice-president with his committee, co-operating with the associate director of the Training Union, should secure from the church roll the names of all the *members of the church* seventeen to twenty-four years of age. Also the church members of the Young People's department and the Young People's classes in the Sunday school should be added to this list. Likewise, the results of the religious census of the community may be utilized for building up the membership of the union. Again, at the evening preaching service young people often attend who are not affiliated with the church, but who might be reached for the church and for the union. Their names and addresses should be secured and added to the above list.

The information from all the above sources should be divided equally among the members of the membership committee and a constant and persistent visitation should be maintained to reach all of them for the union.

The pastor of the church, the president of the union, and the group captains should heartily co-operate with the vice-president and the membership committee in bringing all eligible young people into the union. Until every prospect is enlisted, there should be a systematic visitation carried on each week.

A good membership committee, led by a vigorous vice-president, can keep the union from becoming a clique and transform it into an attractive, winsome organization.

(2) *Holding the new members.*—It is fortunate when a union has a vice-president who understands how to welcome the new members. Some practical suggestions are given for making new members feel at home, which is essential if they are to be held in the Young People's union.

a. New members should be properly classified.—Immediately after a new member has been received into the union, he should be assigned to a group and placed on a committee. The vice-president should see that this is done, though he does not assume the responsibility of doing it himself. It should be done in conference with the president, the counselor, and the other officers involved.

b. New members should be appropriately recognized.—The new member should receive a warm welcome when he joins the Young People's union. He should be publicly introduced by the vice-president. His name should be called and the union should vote him in heartily as though he were really wanted. Of course, care should be exercised and timid people should not be embarrassed on account of undue attention.

c. New members should be supplied with the literature. —The secretary or someone specially designated should supply each new member with a quarterly and other necessary material needed to do the work. The programs should be explained to him and he should be assigned a part on the next program to be rendered by his group. Care should be exercised and difficult parts should not be given to inexperienced new members. The Bible readers' course should always be explained and the daily readings for the week pointed out.

d. New members should be asked to remain for the preaching service.—The vice-president and group captain should see that each new member is asked to remain for the preaching service, and someone should be designated to sit with him if he is a stranger. At the close of the service he should be introduced to the pastor, the director, and the associate director.

The membership committee is responsible for securing the attendance of all the Young People's union members at the evening preaching service. The Standard of Excellence requires that the union shall promote attendance upon the preaching service.

If courteous, sympathetic attention is given to new members at the beginning of their connection with the union they will learn to love and appreciate it. They will be interested in the work and be regular in their attendance and faithful in the discharge of all duties assigned to them.

It is unreasonable to expect strange young people to fall desperately in love with a cold, exclusive, selfish union. Let the membership committee be alert, thoughtful, and attentive to new members and the absentee list in the union will grow beautifully less, as the absentee habit is usually contracted at the very beginning of one's Young People's union experience. However, no matter how thoughtful and careful of new members the union may be, there will always be members who are irregular in their attendance. Let us consider what should be done for them. This is also the work of the vice-president and the membership committee.

(3) Bringing back absentees

a. Investigate causes for irregular attendance.—The membership committee should seek to determine causes for irregular attendance. In most instances this can be done without asking the direct question. Sometimes the union may be at fault. Perhaps the union has not used the absentee member as it should; perhaps the officers have not been attentive to his needs; and there may be other reasons. In any case, if the union is at fault, the vice-president should strive to see that the condition is corrected.

On the other hand, if the absentee member is at fault, the vice-president and membership committee should consider it an opportunity, in patience and love, to help this member see the value of the Young People's union program and to help him develop spiritually.

b. When and how should absentees be followed up. —Immediately. Early the morning following the weekly meeting the vice-president and his committee should get in touch with all members who were absent. No fault-finders or critics should be members of the membership committee. All inquiries and interviews with absentee members should be made with a desire to help and bless. Let the absentee be assured that he was missed and that his presence is desired because the union needs him.

In difficult cases the vice-president and group captains should give personal attention and sometimes, no doubt, the president could well afford to give some time to the matter of visiting absentees. He will be able to win some of them back by his personal efforts.

c. When should the names of absentees be dropped. —The membership committee backed by the group captains should assume responsibility for the attendance of every member of the union and under no circumstances should they consider erasing the name of a member so long as there is a possibility of inducing him to return. Emphasis should be placed upon the worth of the individual, and individual reports should concern the officers more than group averages. Group reports are important and good, and group averages are not to be neglected, but at no time, for even a moment, should the welfare of the individual be sacrificed for a "good report" of the group as a whole.

Let this be made a matter of deepest concern by the president, the vice-president, the entire membership committee, and the group captains. Let them cultivate a spirit of sympathy and patience with members who are irregular in their attendance upon the meetings of the union, and let them utilize these occasional opportunities for the purpose of helping and blessing these young people.

(4) *Encouraging members to be on time.*—Another duty of the membership committee is to urge all members to be on time at the weekly meeting. The names of those who are late should be gotten each Sunday from the secretary, so that they may be called or seen during the week.

(5) *Building up preaching attendance.*—The vice-president should get from the secretary every Sunday a list of those not attending preaching service and assign them to the membership committee to be visited or called during the week. "Every member attending evening preaching service" should be the goal of this committee.

(6) *The vice-president and the monthly officers' council.*—The vice-president should attend the monthly officers' council and help plan all the work of his union for the next month. He will submit to the council, in writing, his plans for the work of his committee. A review and plan sheet is suggested herewith for that purpose.

VICE-PRESIDENT'S MONTHLY REVIEW AND PLAN SHEET

.... Union

SUBMITTED TO OFFICERS' COUNCIL

For Month of.., 19.....

1. Names of membership committee members

   Group one ....

   Group two ....

   Group three ....

   Group four ....

2. Were assignments of work made to all these committee members the past month? ....

   What work did they report on these assignments?.....................

   ....

3. Plans for next month

   (1) Plans for promoting attendance:

   (a) Visitation of absentees ....

   ....

   (b) Encouraging promptness ....

   ....

   (c) Winning new members ....

   ....

   (2) Plans for building preaching attendance ....

   ....

   (3) Plans for building prayer meeting attendance......................

   ....

   ....

   ....

   (4) Other plans ....

   ....

   ....

   .... Vice-President

   .... Union

II. THE MISSIONARY LEADER

It is well understood that the missionary leader is chairman of the missionary committee, and is entrusted with the important work of bringing the Young People's union face to face with the missionary situation, both from a worldwide and denominational viewpoint.

In view of this task it is well to suggest that the missionary leader should be one filled with missionary zeal and love for lost people.

The Standard of Excellence requires that the missionary committee shall promote all the activities of the union in the field of stewardship and missions. These activities are outlined here.

1. Education in Missions

(1) *Monthly missionary programs.*—The last program in the quarterly each month is a missionary subject. Once each month, twelve times each year, the young people study missions. The studies are confined largely to the missionary operations of Southern Baptists.

These programs are varied from year to year to meet the needs. The missionary leader should co-operate with the group captains in making these programs attractive and helpful. He should provide maps of the different fields, have attractive and striking posters made, be on the lookout for illustrations of all kinds from all available sources and see that copies of *The Commission, Southern Baptist Home Missions,* and *The Baptist Training Union Magazine* are in the hands of all the officers and the chairmen of all the committees at least.

(2) *Mission study class.*—The chairman of the missionary committee, in co-operation with the pastor, director, and president, should also see that mission study courses are offered. Plans should be made early for such classes. The young people should be enlisted and a suitable person should be engaged as teacher.

The class should be conducted each evening during the week from Monday to Friday, inclusive, with two class periods each evening of forty-five minutes each, with an address, perhaps, between the classes. The addresses could be arranged to cover all phases of benevolent and missionary work of Southern Baptists at one time. At another time, the work of the Home Mission Board could be covered. At still another time, the work of Southern Baptists in foreign lands could be covered. In this way our young people would, in a short time, be well informed concerning the plans and purposes of Southern Baptists to give the gospel to the whole world, as Christ commanded.

The mission study class may be taken in connection with the church school of missions. One credit on missions is granted in the Young People's Union Study Course. Write to the Training Union Department of the Baptist Sunday School Board, or to the state Training Union department, for the list of electives from which the book on missions may be selected.

2. Educate and Enlist in Scriptural Giving

(1) *Educate.*—The Young People's union is not a money-raising organization, but its business is to educate and train the young people to give as church members to all the objects fostered by their church, according to the Bible plan of giving. There are many ways in which the missionary leader and missionary committee may educate the young people in Bible giving.

To be sure, the young people are not able to make large contributions to causes now, but they will be able to do this later. The young people are the material from which the large givers must be developed. The way to have large givers in our churches is to train the small givers to give as they are prospered of God. If the young people are trained to be faithful in returning to God that which rightfully belongs to him out of their small incomes, they will be faithful in doing the same when their incomes are large. "He that is faithful in that which is least is faithful also in much" (Luke 16:10).

In addition to the weekly meeting subjects and the study course books bearing on this question, the missionary leader should distribute systematically among the young people the many fine leaflets and booklets on giving, stewardship, and tithing.

He should keep on hand an unlimited supply of literature on the great questions and display it attractively before the eyes of the young people and frequently call their attention to it.

Tracts on stewardship and tithing may be ordered from your state mission board. Write and ask what is available.

Attractive stewardship tracts are published by the Baptist Sunday School Board, Nashville, Tennessee.

"Farmer Brown's Conversion to the Doctrine of Stewardship" and "The Trial of the Robbers," two plays in tract form, may be secured from the state Baptist Training Union secretary. They are free.

(2) *Enlist.*—The Standard of Excellence requires that the union shall seek to enlist all its members to give systematically of their means to the causes fostered by the church. Every member of the union should be interviewed personally each year by the finance committee for the purpose of securing his subscription to the budget for the ensuing year. This is a duty the church owes to the young people and is often neglected by the deacons and finance committee, because the young people, as a rule, are not large givers.

The missionary leader should call the attention of the president to this matter and together they should secure the subscription of each member of the union, whether the amount is large or small.

The missionary leader and missionary committee should not stop until every member of the union has subscribed to the church budget. This should usually be done at the time the every-member canvass is made by the church.

3. *Plan and Conduct Practical Missionary Activities*

Soul-winning is the primary and fundamental missionary activity. The missionary committee should seek to win every associate member who is not a Christian, and then to lead all the members of the union to do this work in the Sunday school and everywhere.

The missionary leader and missionary committee should also plan and enlist the whole union in practical missionary work, such as visiting the sick and shut-ins, rendering programs in jails, hospitals, and other institutions. They should also plan and conduct extension work

---

MISSIONARY LEADER'S MONTHLY REVIEW AND PLAN SHEET

.... Union

SUBMITTED TO OFFICERS' COUNCIL

For Month of..., 19.....

1. Names of missionary committee members

    Group one ....

    Group two ....

    Group three ....

    Group four ....

2. Were assignments of work made to all these committee members the past month? ....

    What work did they report on these assignments? ....

    ....

3. Plans for next month ....

    (1) Plans for education of members in stewardship and missions ......

    ....

    ....

    (2) Plans for enlisting tithers..

    ....

    (3) Plans for enlisting members in systematic giving to the church ..

    ....

    ....

    (4) Plans for helping group captain with the missionary program .....

    ....

    ....

    (5) Plans for practical missionary activities ....

    ....

    ....Missionary Leader

    ....Union

in other churches, helping to organize new Young People's unions, conduct study courses, render missionary programs, and do other helpful service.

4. *Plan Brief Missionary Feature for Weekly Meeting*

As is indicated in the suggested Young People's union schedule on page 59, the missionary leader should have approximately 3 minutes to present a missionary feature on Sunday evening. This is a brief time, of course, but it is an important opportunity. The time may be used to emphasize some part of the work for which he is responsible. For example, he may give reviews of missionary articles and books, present stewardship tracts and testimonies, and emphasize soul-winning through testimonies, tracts, and by encouraging daily prayer for the lost. The missionary leader should meet with the program committee during the first part of the general officers' council to perfect plans for the mission emphases.

5. *The Missionary Leader and the Monthly Officers' Council*

The missionary leader should attend the monthly officers' council of his union and help plan all the work of the union for the next month. At this meeting he will submit in writing the plans for the work of the missionary committee for the next month. See Missionary Leader's Monthly Review and Plan Sheet on preceding page.

OUTLINE

I. THE VICE-PRESIDENT
   1. Presides in the Absence of the President
   2. Chairman of the Membership Committee
      (1) The membership committee
      (2) The Young People's union membership

3. Work of the Membership Committee
   (1) Reaching new members
   (2) Holding the new members
   (3) Bringing back absentees
   (4) Encouraging members to be on time
   (5) Building up preaching attendance
   (6) The vice-president and the monthly officers' council

II. THE MISSIONARY LEADER

1. Education in Missions
   (1) Monthly missionary programs
   (2) Mission study class
2. Educate and Enlist in Scriptural Giving
   (1) Educate
   (2) Enlist
3. Plan and Conduct Practical Missionary Activities
4. Plan Brief Missionary Feature for Weekly Meeting
5. The Missionary Leader and the Monthly Officers' Council

CHAPTER 6

The Secretary

THE SECRETARY of the Young People's union is responsible for the records. He should be one who loves bookkeeping and has a deep appreciation of the value of records in building a great organization. Records are not an end in themselves, but a means to getting better work done and measuring achievements in training.

I. THE VALUE OF RECORDS

1. *Reliable Records Measure Progress*

The business of the Young People's union is to train its members in church membership. With this in view, it strives to have each one present at the weekly meetings, on time, having read his Bible daily, and having studied the lesson. The effort is also made to enlist each one in taking the study courses, taking part on the programs, giving to the church, and attending the preaching services. The Young People's union succeeds in proportion to its effectiveness in enlisting its members in these activities. Reliable records show whether or not this is being done, from week to week, and from year to year, in the case of each member and in the union as a whole.

2. *Good Records Stimulate Activity*

An individual's past record may be used to great advantage to spur him on to greater activity in the future. For this reason, an accurate record of each member should be kept as long as he is in the union. Monthly individual reports should be given to each member by the secretary. Likewise, the weekly and monthly reports of the secretary to the union should show the exact standing of the groups and the union. At all times the ideal achievement should be held up so that the actual record of the union may be compared with it. The secretary has a splendid opportunity to stimulate greater activity by the proper exploitation of records.

3. Accurate Records Cultivate Thoroughness

Well-kept records cultivate thoroughness in the Young People's union. There is fine business training for the secretary in keeping accurate records. Orderliness and system may be promoted in all the work of the union by keeping accurate records and making the right kind of reports. Thoroughness is a much-needed quality in all phases of church work. There is too much lack of definiteness in most church activities. Many of the members think of their church work as a side issue, and do not put into it their best of time, talent, and energy. Haphazard methods result. The time to overcome this is in youth. The place is the Young People's union.

II. THE EIGHT POINTS STATED AND EXPLAINED

1. *Present, 10 per cent.*—This point refers to attendance upon the weekly meeting.

2. *On Time, 10 per cent.*—If the meeting opens at 6:30, a member must be in his place at exactly 6:30 or before or he will lose ten points from his weekly grade. In Training Unions having an opening assembly, or in departments having an opening assembly, this refers to the time set for the assembly to begin.

3. *Studied Lesson, 15 per cent.*—The third point refers to studying the whole program for the weekly meeting every week. It does not refer just to studying the assignment to be discussed when one's group renders the program.

4. *Taking Part on Program, 15 per cent.*—This point refers to taking some part on the program aside from

the congregational singing every time one's group renders a program. The part may be making a talk, reading the Scripture, or rendering special music. If a member serves on the program when his group renders the program, he is entitled to this grade every Sunday until the next time his group renders the program. If he fails to take a part, he loses the grade every Sunday until the next time he has an opportunity to serve. Borrowing is discouraged. Reading from quarterly is not counted.

Great care should be exercised in the matter of using on the program young people who are not Christians. The Standard of Excellence does not require that associate members be used at all. They should never be used for any part which presupposes that they are Christians.

5. *Study Course, 10 per cent.*—To make this grade a member must complete every twelve months at least one approved Training Union Study Course textbook, as recommended by the Baptist Sunday School Board. The grade is given every Sunday for twelve months following the date the course was completed.

6. *Daily Bible Reading, 15 per cent.*—To make this grade in his weekly report, it is necessary that a member shall have read daily, every day in the week, the readings as published in the Training Union daily Bible readers' course. No exceptions allowed. The Standard of Excellence requires the union to follow the course as published in *Baptist Young People* or *Baptist Married Young People*.

7. *Attending Preaching, 10 per cent.*—When a member marks his individual report, he is entitled to 10 per cent on point number seven if he attends the evening preaching service of the church in which he is a Training Union member on the same day in which the record is marked.

In no case would members of the church where the Training Union is located be allowed credit on this point for attending preaching in a church of another denomination, or in another Baptist church, unless sent by the

Training Union to do extension work. Credit should not be given for attending the morning preaching service except in churches where there is no evening service. In churches that have preaching only once or twice a month, this grade would be allowed every Sunday from one preaching day to the next, if the member was present.

8. *Giving, 15 per cent.*—For all members, active and associate, this refers to giving of one's means systematically, according to the church plan, into the church treasury, to all local expenses of the church, and to missions and benevolences. If a church does not have a plan for raising its funds, the union may secure an offering for church support and missions every Sunday from its members, and give this credit to all who participate.

The missionary leader and missionary committee are responsible for enlisting every member of the union in giving to the church. A strong effort should also be made to enlist every member as a tither.

NOTE.—*Giving credit to absentees*. The question is frequently raised as to whether or not any credit on the records should be given to an absentee. In the case of one who can give a providential reason for being absent, and who signs his record and brings, telephones it to someone, or sends it to the secretary by the time of the weekly meeting, whatever grade he makes should be given to him. Of course, he cannot make the grades on "Present" and "On Time" unless he is sent by his union, general officers, or association to some other church to do extension work and is present and on time in that Training Union's weekly meeting. The same provision should be made for a member who is visiting in some other community too far away for him to get to his own Training Union, provided he attends the Training Union there, and signs his record and sends or telephones it to his own secretary. In all cases the written record shall be required before credit is given. In all cases in which the absent member is visiting some other Training Union meeting at the same time his own Training Union meets, he should sign his record at the meeting and turn it in to his secretary afterwards. The secretary may then make the proper adjustment of the individual's records. In cases in which the absent member is not to be present at some other Training Union, he may send in his signed record to his secretary before the meeting, so that it may be included in the weekly report. In no cases should credit be given unless the absent member can give a providential reason for being absent.

III. Operating the Eight Point Record System

The Eight Point Record System is not difficult to operate if the suggestions given here are followed:

1. *Preparation*

(1) *Study the system and equipment.*—A partial list is given here:

Eight Point Individual Report (weekly envelopes or slips)
Eight Point Individual Report for Three Months
Training Union Visitor's Record
Individual Union Secretary's Weekly Report
Weekly Report of Group Captain (slips)
Group Captain's Record Books
Secretary's Record Book
President's Notebook
Training Union Prospect Record
Training Union Visitation Assignment and Report
Baptist Training Union Classification Slip
Young People's Union Monthly Individual Achievement Report (Order from Baptist Book Store serving your area.)

Each union will want to co-operate with the general plan for the Training Union. The union secretary should confer with the general secretary about this plan.

Each Training Union should order a catalogue of supplies from the nearest Baptist Book Store. All prices are given in this catalogue.

(2) *Explain the records to the union.*—An individual report should be put into the hands of each member, and the secretary should then explain each point, as described in the discussion above. It would be well to put these points, with their values, on a large chart, and put it on the wall in the meeting place. The system cannot be operated successfully unless all understand.

(3) *Classify the membership of the union.*—Every member should sign the classification slip, so the secretary may have the necessary information concerning each one for permanent record. If the church has the Baptist

---

TRAINING UNION CLASSIFICATION RECORD
To be filled out by each new member

Name_____Date_____

Residence Address_____Phone_____

Business Address_____Phone_____

Age_____Birthday: Month_____Day_____Year_____

Christian?_____Denomination_____Church Member?_____

Name and address of church_____

Have you ever been a member of Training Union?_____

If under 17 years of age, enter this information:
Parents' Name_____

Father Christian?_____Member What Church?_____Where?_____

Mother Christian?_____Member What Church?_____Where?_____

Assigned to
_____Unit_____Department
{ Leader or
{ President
_____
_____ Department Director

Three copies of this classification record should be made: one copy for the secretary of the unit, one copy for the department secretary, and one copy for the general secretary.

FORM TU-1020 EIGHT POINT RECORD SYSTEM. BAPTIST SUNDAY SCHOOL BOARD, NASHVILLE, TENN. COPYRIGHT, 1951, BSSB

Training Union, a duplicate classification slip should be given to the associate director, who is classification officer. (See above.)

EIGHT POINT INDIVIDUAL REPORT

"A workman that needeth not to be ashamed" (2 Tim. 2:15)

Name_____Phone_____

Address_____

Member of Group_____Visitor_____

Present 10%	On Time 10%	Studied Lesson 15%	On Program 15%	Study Course 10%	Daily Bible Reading 15%	Attending Preaching 10%	Giving to Church 15%	Contacts	Grade

FORM TU-1030 EIGHT POINT RECORD SYSTEM. BAPTIST SUNDAY SCHOOL BOARD, NASHVILLE, TENN., COPYRIGHT, 1951, BSSB

---

2. *Keeping the Records in the Secretary's Record Book*

(1) *A record of each individual.*—It is important above everything else in keeping records to have available at all times an accurate record of every member of the union. If this is to be done, two things are necessary:

TRAINING UNION VISITOR'S RECORD

Name_____Date_____

Residence Address_____Phone_____

Business Address_____Phone_____

Christian?_____Denomination _____Church Member?_____

Name and location of church_____

Have you ever been a member of Training Union?_____

Visiting in _____Union _____Department

Comments:_____

FORM TU-1015 EIGHT POINT RECORD SYSTEM. BAPTIST SUNDAY SCHOOL BOARD, NASHVILLE, TENN., COPYRIGHT, 1951, BSSB

---

a. Secure an individual report every Sunday.—It is best to have all the members of the union fill out these reports at the same time. Let the secretary give to the group captains the number of envelopes or slips necessary for each group. The group captains distribute them. At the proper time the president should announce that the reports are to be filled out. Have plenty of extra pen-

---

EIGHT POINT INDIVIDUAL REPORT FOR THREE MONTHS
To be used every Sunday for one quarter
"A workman that needeth not to be ashamed" (2 Tim. 2:15)

Name_____Address_____Phone_____

Group_____Union_____Department_____

Quarter_____Year_____

Month		FIRST MONTH					SECOND MONTH					THIRD MONTH				
Sundays		1	2	3	4	5	1	2	3	4	5	1	2	3	4	5
Present	10%															
On Time	10%															
Studied Lesson	15%															
On Program	15%															
Study Course	10%															
Daily Bible Reading	15%															
Attending Preaching	10%															
Giving to Church	15%															
Weekly Grades																
Total Contacts																

Monthly Grades: First____ Second____ Third____ Quarterly Grade_____
Note.—This record should be transferred each week by the secretary to the union secretary's record book.
FORM TU-1040G EIGHT POINT RECORD SYSTEM. BAPTIST SUNDAY SCHOOL BOARD, NASHVILLE, TENN. COPYRIGHT. 1951. BSSB
(OVER)

There is also an individual record card for twelve months.

cils for those who do not have them. Explain that the grade is to be marked opposite each point, or a cross mark opposite the points not attained. Each member will then add the grades on the points. The sum is the individual's grade for the week. The individual reports are then passed to the group captains, and the meeting proceeds. The group captains, after making up their weekly reports (see page 101) and marking their record books, should turn the individual reports over to the secretary.

Some unions prefer to use the individual record card for securing the records. This card lasts three months.

ADDITIONAL INFORMATION

Name_____ Date_____

Residence Address_____ Phone_____

Business Address_____ Phone_____

Age_____ Birthday: Month_____ Day_____ Year_____

Christian?_____ Denomination_____ Church Member?_____

Name and address of church_____

Have you ever been a member of Training Union?_____

If under 17 years of age, enter this information:

Parents' Name_____

Father Christian?_____ Member What Church?_____ Where?_____

Mother Christian?_____ Member What Church?_____ Where?_____

(Back side of card shown on preceding page.)

b. Keep individual record of every member in secretary's record book.—The secretary should keep a roll of the members, arranged alphabetically, by groups, in the record book. The individual reports should be carried home and there copied into the record book as early in the week as possible.

(2) *Record of the union organization.*—The secretary's record book provides spaces for keeping a record of all officers and their attendance upon the monthly officers'

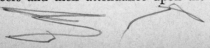

council. It also provides spaces for keeping a record of the committees. The pages to be used in keeping a record of all members, by groups, immediately follow the pages for committee records. The book, if kept properly, lasts one year.

(3) *Record of weekly blackboard reports.*—Under "Making Reports" will be found a diagram of the secretary's weekly report for the blackboard. Every weekly report should be copied into the secretary's record book in the spaces provided for that purpose. Spaces are also provided for making quarterly summaries of these weekly reports.

(4) *Minutes.*—Pages are provided in the secretary's record book for keeping minutes of all business transacted by the union in regular meetings or officers' councils.

3. Making Reports

(1) *The weekly report on the blackboard.*—Concerning the weekly report, note carefully the following points:

a. The group captains should make up the totals from the individual reports, and make a report to the secretary.

As soon as the group captains mark their record books they should turn over to the secretary the individual report slips (or cards) and the group captain's report.

The secretary, or an assistant, should collect all reports from the captains and carry them to the secretary's table.

In smaller unions this step may be omitted with the individual report slips going directly to the secretary. In such a case, after the union secretary has recorded each member's record, the individual record slips should be given to the group captains.

b. The secretary should make the report on the blackboard.

This report should be transferred to the secretary's record book for permanent record.

c. A copy of the weekly report should be sent by the secretary to the department secretary or to the general secretary if the Training Union is not departmentized.

d. Figuring the grades. The group grade is found by dividing the sum of the individual grades by the number on the group. The grade of the union is found by dividing the sum of the individual grades by the number of members in the union, president and counselor included.

The quarterly average grade is found by adding the weekly grades and dividing the sum by the number of Sundays in the quarter.

The secretary should work on all records at a table in the rear of the room. He should put the report on the blackboard there, and bring it forward and hang it on the wall when the president calls for the report.

(2) *Report on absentees, those not "On Time," those not reading the Bible, and those not "Attending Preaching."*—One of the duties of the secretary is to make up a list of absentees and those not on time and those not attending the evening preaching service every Sunday and give it to the vice-president and membership committee at the close of the meeting. Likewise, a list of those not reading the Bible should be given to the Bible readers' leader. There is no use in making a record of our failures unless we are going to do something about it. The secretary should be prepared at all times to give all officers and committees just the information they need to do their work intelligently.

(3) *Monthly reports*

a. At the close of each month the secretary may give to each member of the union a report as listed on page 100. An honor roll of those making 100 per cent may be posted in the meeting place.

b. The secretary should make a monthly report to the union in the monthly officers' council as required by the

---

MONTHLY REPORT OF SECRETARY

TO MONTHLY OFFICERS' COUNCIL

.... **Union**

For Month of.., 19....

Averages for the month:

Average enrolment.................. Average attendance..............

Average number on time..................... Average number studied lesson............... Number on program...............Number completed study course......................... Average number daily Bible readers........................... Average number attending preaching.................. Average number giving to church................

Grade for the month...................... Group grades for the month:

Group one ....

Group two ....

Group three ....

Group four ....

Number of members making grade of 70% or above for past month....

....

Was union Standard the past month?.................... If any points were lacking, name them, and tell which officers and committees are responsible ....

....

....

.... Secretary

.... Union

Standard of Excellence. This report should be a summary of the weekly reports made on the blackboard. A suggested form for this is submitted herewith.

(4) *Application for Standard award.*—When the union has maintained Standard rating for a quarter, application for the Standard award should be made in duplicate to the state Training Union secretary. The union secretary should fill out the form and give it to the president. Application blanks may be secured from the state Training Union secretary or from the Training Union Department, Baptist Sunday School Board.

Young People's Union
MONTHLY INDIVIDUAL ACHIEVEMENT REPORT
To be filled out for each member by the secretary

Report of _____

For Month of _____ 19___ Number of Sundays_____

"Study to shew thyself approved unto God, a workman that needeth not to be ashamed" (2 Tim. 2:15)

Number of Sundays making each point and total grade for month

Present 10%	On Time 10%	Studied Lesson 15%	On Program 15%	Study Course 10%	Daily Bible Reading 15%	Attending Preaching 10%	Giving to Church 15%	GRADE FOR MONTH

NOTE.—In order for your union to maintain Standard rating, at least two thirds of its members must make individual average grades for the quarter of at least 70% on the Eight Point Record System.

Signed _____

Secretary

FORM TU-1425 EIGHT POINT RECORD SYSTEM. BAPTIST SUNDAY SCHOOL BOARD, NASHVILLE, TENN., COPYRIGHT, 1951, BSSB

REQUEST FOR TAKING NAME FROM ROLL
To be made to executive committee

Unit _____ Department _____ Date _____

Please give permission to take from roll _____
(Name)

Because _____

Date last visited _____

Approved by executive committee   Signed by _____

Date _____ For _____
Unit

_____
Associate Department Director

_____
Associate Director

FORM TU-1155 EIGHT POINT RECORD SYSTEM. BAPTIST SUNDAY SCHOOL BOARD, NASHVILLE, TENN., COPYRIGHT, 1951, BSSB

WEEKLY REPORT OF GROUP CAPTAIN

NOTE.—The group captain should make up the totals for this report from the individual reports of the group members, figure the grade of the group, mark the number making 70% or above, mark contacts made, and hand to the secretary. He should then mark his record book and also give the individual reports to the secretary.

Date _____ 19_____

Union_____Group _____

	Totals
Enrolled_____	
Absent_____	
Present 10% _____	
On Time 10%_____	
Studied Lesson 15%_____	
On Program 15% _____	
Study Course 10% _____	
Daily Bible Readers 15% _____	
Attending Preaching 10% _____	
Giving to Church 15%_____	
Total Present_____	
Total Contacts_____	
Group Grade_____	
No. Making 70% or Above____	

NOTE.—The group grade is found by dividing the sum of the individual grades by the number enrolled in the group, or by multiplying the totals of each point by the value of that point, adding the eight products thus obtained, and dividing the sum by the enrolment of the group.

Signed _____
Group Captain

FORM TU-1105 EIGHT POINT RECORD SYSTEM. BAPTIST SUNDAY SCHOOL BOARD. NASHVILLE,TENN.. COPYRIGHT, 1951, BSSB

OUTLINE

I. THE VALUE OF RECORDS

    1. Reliable Records Measure Progress

    2. Good Records Stimulate Activity

    3. Accurate Records Cultivate Thoroughness

II. THE EIGHT POINTS STATED AND EXPLAINED

III. OPERATING THE EIGHT POINT RECORD SYSTEM

    1. Preparation

        (1) Study the system and equipment

        (2) Explain the records to the union

        (3) Classify the membership of the union

    2. Keeping the Records in the Secretary's Record Book

        (1) A record of each individual

        (2) Record of the union organization

        (3) Record of weekly blackboard reports

        (4) Minutes

    3. Making Reports

        (1) The weekly report on the blackboard

        (2) Report on absentees, those not "On Time," those not reading the Bible, and those not "Attending Preaching"

        (3) Monthly reports

        (4) Application for Standard award

CHAPTER 7

The Social Leader, Song Leader, and Pianist

I. THE SOCIAL LEADER

The work of the social leader and social committee is to direct the social activities of the Young People's union. In the selection of the social leader, his qualifications for doing this work should be considered.

There are so many good books offering practical plans for the social life of the young people that we shall not attempt here to present methods for entertaining young people, but simply make a few suggestions concerning the duties of the social leader and social committee.

The social activities of the Young People's union, Sunday school Young People's classes, and all the other organizations of the church for this age group should be co-ordinated, and there should be no conflict or confusion at any point or at any time with any of the work of any of these organizations. The pastor of the church, the educational director, if the church has one, the superintendent of the Sunday school, the president of the Woman's Missionary Union, and the director of the Training Union should meet frequently to formulate and agree upon policies and plans of work in order that all these agencies may function together harmoniously.

The Standard of Excellence requires at least one social each quarter, but permits combination socials, planned and conducted in co-operation with other church organizations, to count not more than twice a year in meeting this requirement.

The social committee is composed of the social leader,

103

chairman, with a member from each one of the groups on the committee. In small unions the chairman may represent the committee in his own group. The work of the social committee is not by any means confined to giving and directing parties, but there is something for this committee to do every day in the week. Let us see what some of these duties are.

1. Greet Members and Visitors at Weekly Meetings

The social leader should have his committee present at the weekly meeting of the union fifteen to thirty minutes ahead of time. As the members and visitors arrive, they should meet and greet them and make everybody feel at ease.

2. Greet the Young People at the Evening Preaching Service

The social committee can do a great deal toward building the fellowship among union members and good will toward the union by taking advantage of the opportunities offered at the evening preaching service. If there are young people at the service who are not members of the Training Union, the social committee should make it a point to cultivate their friendship. Likewise, a friendly greeting for the union members can help to build a spirit of friendliness and fellowship.

3. Co-operate in the Work of Visitation

The social leader should earnestly line up his committee with the membership committee and engage with this committee in its work of visitation. Undoubtedly a good social committee is the greatest ally, humanly speaking, that a membership committee can have.

The social committee should be definitely concerned about the absentees of the union. Find out why they are absent and give them special attention. In cases of sickness and need, material aid may be given by the social committee.

In each special visitation conducted by the membership committee, the social committee can render an invaluable service by planning a social feature to be held during the report period at the close of the visitation. This social feature may simply be refreshments, or a stunt, or in some instances planned games. The object is, of course, to build the fellowship of the union.

4. Plan the Socials

The social leader with his committee should direct the social life of the Young People's union. Certainly this committee should invoke the aid and co-operation of the pastor of the church, the educational director, Training Union director, the president of the Young People's union, and the group captains. The Standard of Excellence calls for at least one social quarterly. However, it is probable that the average union should have more than one social each quarter. Certainly these socials should include all the members of the union and all the members of the church who should belong to the union. Also, the members of the union may invite their friends to the socials occasionally.

(1) *Plan for variety.*—The social committee will want to make certain that a varied social program is presented for the young people. There are many opportunities for variety suggested by the seasons of the year, by special holidays, and by the interests of the young people.

Many unions and departments have found it advisable to have some social features provided annually. For example, an annual picnic and an annual sweetheart banquet are characteristic of many unions and departments. Throughout the year other social features are promoted to add variety and "spice" to the social program.

(2) *Plan well.*—The social committee has an obligation to see that all socials are well-planned. The importance of a wholesome social program should lead the committee to plan every detail carefully.

Many helps are available to the social committee for

planning. The Recreation Service of the Baptist Sunday School Board provides free leaflets on every phase of recreation. There are social suggestions in *The Baptist Training Union Magazine*. There are also many good books. Some of these books are:

> *The Pleasure Chest*, Eisenberg
> *The Party Game Book*, Mulac and Holmes
> *Choice Socials for Young People*, Pylant
> *Choice Sunday Night Fellowships*, Pylant
> *Choice Social Programs for Students*, Pylant
> *Playtime*, Pylant
> *Phunology*, Harbin
> *The Fun Encyclopedia*, Harbin
> *The Cokesbury Game Book*, Depew
> *The Cokesbury Stunt Book*, Depew
> *A Handbook for Church Recreation Leaders*, Maston
> *Geister Games*, Edna Geister
> *Handy Games*, Rohrbough

(3) *Plan for co-operation with department and general socials.*—Every Young People's union should co-operate with the Young People's department director and the Training Union director on general social features in which they are included. In many instances the two annual features suggested in section 1 are department or Training Union features rather than union features. The social committee of the union, in all such cases, should co-operate in making these social functions a success.

(4) *Plan a fellowship hour.*—Many Young People's unions and departments have found it advisable to promote a fellowship hour for young people at the close of the evening preaching service. In most instances young people who attend the evening service and are not members of the Young People's union are also invited to participate in the fellowship hour.

Some churches prefer to have the Young People's fellowship hour prior to Training Union. In such cases a snack supper is served to the young people before they go to their departments or unions.

The fellowship hour is suggested for churches where it meets a definite need. It is never suggested that attendance at the fellowship hour be promoted as it would for Sunday school or Training Union or any other of the regular church services. Some Young People's unions have found it advisable to promote this feature during certain seasons of the year and discontinue it during others. A good rule to follow is: Promote the fellowship hour as long as it meets a felt need and serves a definite purpose.

What type of program should be planned? Here again a varied program should be provided. Variety may be obtained by including some of the following suggestions: simple fellowship games, a program of singing, a general discussion on some topic of interest, helpful films, or testimony meetings. In some cases where a program in *Baptist Young People* or *Baptist Married Young People* has attracted particular attention and there has not been enough time for discussion, the discussion may be continued during the fellowship hour with a competent leader, such as the pastor or educational director, leading.

The fellowship hour should not be long. It usually varies in length from a half hour to an hour.

It is always advisable to close the fellowship hour with a brief devotional thought. Many young people's groups have found that the friendship circle can accomplish this. After the young people are gathered in a circle, several verses of Scripture may be quoted, a prayer can be offered, and the friendship circle closed with the singing of "Blest Be the Tie."

It is usually advisable to have the fellowship period for the Young People's department separate from such programs for other departments. Young people like to feel that some features are planned especially for them.

Since the fellowship hour comes on Sunday evening it should be considered a promotional project for the Young

SOCIAL LEADER'S MONTHLY REVIEW AND PLAN SHEET

.... **Union**

SUBMITTED TO OFFICERS' COUNCIL

For Month of..., 19....

1. Names of social committee members

   Group one ....

   Group two ....

   Group three ....

   Group four ....

2. Were assignments of work made to all these committee members the past month? ....

   What work did they report on these assignments?...................

   ....

3. Plans for next month

   (1) Plans for social. Date.................. Place....................

   Remarks ....

   (2) Plans for visitation of sick...

   ....

   (3) Plans for cultivation of good fellowship in weekly meetings.......

   ....

   ....

   (4) Other plans ....

   ....

   .... Social Leader

   .... Union

People's union and department. It is an opportunity for the church to minister to the needs of young people through the Young People's union.

(5) *A closing word.*—What young people do in their social life has a great effect upon their spiritual life. One cannot engage in doubtful amusements and at the same time maintain a high spiritual plane. In other words, one cannot be wrong in his social life and right in his spiritual life. Likewise, the kind of social pleasures the young people engage in will manifest itself outwardly in their spiritual walk and conversation.

MONTHLY REVIEW AND PLAN SHEET OF THE SONG LEADER AND PIANIST

.... Union

SUBMITTED TO OFFICERS' COUNCIL

For Month of..., 19....

1. Review of past month

   (1) Number of meetings in which music was directed ....

   ....

   (2) Special music planned and given....................................

   (3) Program committee meeting attended............................

   (4) Other work done...

2. Plans for next month

   (1) Special music ....

   ....

   (2) Songs selected for weekly meetings

   First Sunday ....

   Second Sunday ....

   Third Sunday ....

   Fourth Sunday ....

   Fifth Sunday ....

   (3) Other plans ....

   ....

   ...., Chorister

   ...., Pianist

   .... Union

5. The Social Leader and the Monthly Officers' Council

The social leader should attend the monthly officers' council and help plan all the work of the union for the next month. He will submit in writing to the council his plans for the work of the social committee for the coming month. A suggested form for this is submitted herewith. He should also meet with the program committee during the first period of the general officers' council to perfect plans for making the meeting place attractive.

II. Song Leader and Pianist

A song leader and a pianist are recommended for Young People's unions where there is no department or general assembly at the beginning of the Training Union hour. In such cases these officers serve on the program committee and are responsible for maintaining the very finest musical program possible for a Young People's union. The song leader should see that appropriate songs are selected for each program and should co-operate with the president in the opening devotional feature.

Since most Young People's unions do not elect a song leader and a pianist, a complete discussion of the duties of these officers is not given here. Additional information and helps may be obtained in the free tract, "The Chorister and Pianist of the Sunday School and Training Union," prepared by the Church Music Department of the Baptist Sunday School Board.

The song leader and pianist in a Young People's union and other young people who are studying music will be interested in the Church Music Training Course which is promoted by the Church Music Department of the Baptist Sunday School Board and the state music directors. An outline of this course may be obtained by writing to your state Baptist office or to the Baptist Sunday School Board, Nashville, Tennessee.

OUTLINE

I. The Social Leader

1. Greet Members and Visitors at Weekly Meetings
2. Greet the Young People at the Evening Preaching Service
3. Co-operate in the Work of Visitation
4. Plan the Socials
   (1) Plan for variety

    (2) Plan well

    (3) Plan for co-operation with department and general socials

    (4) Plan a fellowship hour

    (5) A closing word

5. The Social Leader and the Monthly Officers' Council

II. SONG LEADER AND PIANIST

CHAPTER 8

The Bible Readers' Leader

THE BIBLE readers' leader is one of the most important officers in the Young People's union. When the nature of his work is considered, it is readily seen that the importance of his position is second to none in the union. He is chairman of the Bible reading committee, and in this capacity is responsible for the Bible readers' course. He is also responsible for aiding in building and maintaining an attractive church library. We thus see that the Bible readers' leader has in large measure the direction of the reading and study of the young people.

Someone has said, "He who plays fast and loose with his thinking, plays fast and loose with his conscience." This raises the important question: Can there be proper mental and spiritual development of our young people unless they do a reasonable amount of the right kind of reading? Here we have close at hand the Holy Bible, the Word of God, and literally thousands of good books in every way suited to the needs of our young people.

This other question: Are our young people reading their Bibles as they should, and do they read, to any appreciable extent, the good books which are so easily accessible? They must read their Bibles. They must read good books.

I. THE DAILY BIBLE READERS' COURSE

The Bible readers' course and the duties of the Bible readers' leader may be clearly set out and understood in the following outline: *First,* the value of the Bible readers' course; *second,* the purpose of the Bible readers' course; *third,* the place of the Bible readers' course; *fourth,* the plan of the Bible readers' course; *fifth,* the method of the Bible readers' course.

1. *The Value of the Bible to the Young Christian*

When we consider what the study of the Bible will do for us, it is strange indeed that Christian people will allow themselves to neglect, even for a day, this great book. While it is true, perhaps, that the Bible is now being read by a greater number of people than at any time in the world's history, at the same time multitudes of Christian people never study the Bible with any degree of purpose or system.

When we estimate the value of the Bible to the life of the Christian and realize how little time is being devoted to its study, we are filled with shame and confusion. Let each young Christian who takes this study make this a very personal matter, and consider seriously what should be his attitude toward his Bible. Let each resolve that he will never spend less than fifteen minutes a day in Bible study and prayer.

(1) *The Bible essential to his spiritual growth.*—Every Christian ought to grow spiritually. The Bible injunction is "Grow in grace, and in the knowledge of our Lord and Saviour Jesus Christ."

Our spiritual growth is largely a matter of our own direction. Chiefest among the means to be employed by us in our spiritual advancement is the study of the Bible. Those who have tried it know from experience that this is true. The Bible also clearly teaches this great truth in many places: "As newborn babes, desire the sincere milk of the word, that ye may grow thereby" (1 Peter 2:2). "I commend you to God, and to the word of his grace, which is able to build you up" (Acts 20:32). "Sanctify them through thy truth: thy word is truth" (John 17:17).

We thus have explicit direction whereby we may grow

into strong men and women in Christ Jesus, and every young Christian who has an ambition to grow more like Christ day by day may realize this holy ambition through personal contact with the Word of God.

(2) *The Bible essential to his happiness.*—All people desire to be happy, though they may differ in their ideas of what happiness is and of what it consists. Young people especially are seeking happiness. Truly every one of them ought to be happy. In fact, God would have us all enjoy life and sing as we go through the world. There is one sure way of attaining this much-desired condition, and that is through studying the Bible. Note what the Bible has to say about this: "The statutes of the Lord are right, rejoicing the heart: the commandment of the Lord is pure, enlightening the eyes. More to be desired are they than gold, yea, than much fine gold: sweeter also than honey and the honeycomb." (Psalm 19:8, 10).

We desire to go a step further in this study and make it clear and plain that unless the young Christian does study his Bible he cannot have in his heart and soul the peace that he longs for and which should be his. He must take it into his heart day by day and assimilate its truths in order to profit from its precepts. The Bible is an all-powerful defensive weapon to the young Christian, a safeguard against sin. The Bible, when hid away in the Christian's heart, is a sin preventive. The psalmist says in Psalm 119:11: "Thy word have I hid in mine heart, that I might not sin against thee."

It is, therefore, all important that Christian people should constantly study their Bibles, as every Christian who neglects the study of the Bible imperils his spiritual growth and his happiness. But this is not all, as we shall see from the next discussion.

(3) *The Bible essential to his usefulness.*—Second Timothy 2:15 enjoins upon us the duty of preparation for Christian service, and indicates that in order to be skilled workmen it is essential that we know how to use

the Word of God. "Study to shew thyself approved unto God, a workman that needeth not to be ashamed, rightly dividing the word of truth." Also 2 Timothy 3:16–17 emphasizes the truth that God's workmen must know how to use the Word of God, which is the Sword of the Spirit, if he would be able skilfully to do the work which God has called him to do. "All scripture is given by inspiration of God, and is profitable for doctrine, for reproof, for correction, for instruction in righteousness: that the man of God may be perfect, thoroughly furnished unto all good works."

It has been said that "the instrument is just as skilful as the one who uses it, be it pen or tongue or sword or broom." This is true.

One worker will make a failure with any kind of an instrument, no matter how good the metal and sharp the edge, because he does not know how to use it. Another worker will make a success, using the same instrument, because he has prepared himself for his work and knows how to use the instrument skilfully.

The Bible is the Christian's weapon, both defensively and offensively. It is a perfect instrument, two-edged and sharp. Every Christian has this instrument close at hand and can use it if he will. Some are using it mightily for God; others wield it occasionally and very indifferently; while in the hands of other soldiers of Christ this instrument is idle. Why this difference? Certainly the trouble is not with the instrument! "For the word of God is quick, and powerful, and sharper than any two-edged sword, piercing even to the dividing asunder of soul and spirit, and of the joints and marrow, and is a discerner of the thoughts and intents of the heart" (Heb. 4:12).

Having seen something of the value of the Bible to the young Christian, let us see how the Bible readers' course helps him to study the Bible and make it purposeful in his life.

2. *The Purpose of the Bible Readers' Course*

The main purpose of the Bible readers' course is to furnish the young people a systematic plan for studying their Bibles. The Bible readers' course provides a simple guide by which the young people may govern their Bible study, which, if followed, will do away with the usual aimless and haphazard way many people have in reading their Bibles.

The young people are busy and need to have provided for them a simple, definite plan by which they can in a connected way, day by day, read their Bibles. The Bible readers' course, as we have it in the Young People's union, admirably meets this need.

3. *The Place of the Bible Readers' Course*

The Bible readers' course occupies first place in the work of the Young People's union. It stands out as the great essential in the education of Baptist young people. The Bible reading committee should see that every member of the union takes advantage of the opportunity it affords to study the Word of God, that he may thus fortify his life against evil and prepare himself to be a valiant soldier of Jesus.

4. *The Plan of the Bible Readers' Course*

The Bible readers' course as offered through the Training Union for private devotions is a five-year course. The first two years are devoted to reading the Bible through by books, giving the first two months of each quarter to Old Testament books and the third month to New Testament books. The next two years are given to reading the Bible by topics. The fifth year presents a special study of the New Testament.

It will be noted that each chapter and verse in the Bible are not read. Choice selections are recommended which make an appeal to young people and which will greatly enrich the lives of young people if they will read them daily and meditate upon what they have read. The suggested daily readings should be considered the minimum amount to be read. Alert young people will want to read much more.

In the quarterly a comment is given on each day's reading and a suggestion is made for the prayer period along with the names of missionaries for the daily prayer list.

5. *The Method of the Bible Readers' Course*

(1) *The Bible readers' leader.*—As stated in the beginning of this chapter the work of having the Bible readers' course made effective is entrusted to the Bible readers' leader. This individual is responsible to the president, to the union, and to the church for having every member of the union to read his Bible daily. This is his main task and he should not shirk it. Let him study his work and follow the instructions below.

(2) *Bible reading committee.*—The Bible readers' leader should have associated with him in his work the Bible reading committee, composed of a member from each group. The member of the committee in each group is definitely charged with the responsibility of having all the members in his group do their Bible readings daily. This makes it a very simple and definite matter and narrows the work of each committeeman to the confines of his own group.

(3) *Group captains.*—Each group captain has as one of his main duties the work of having each member of his group read his Bible. To this end he should co-operate with the Bible readers' leader and the member of the Bible reading committee on his group.

(4) *Quarterlies,* Open Windows, *and* The Bible Reader's Guide and Missionary Prayer Calendar *carry Bible Readers' Course.*—The daily readings are printed in the two quarterlies, in *Open Windows* and in *The Bible Reader's Guide and Missionary Prayer Calendar*. The comments and suggestions for the daily prayer for each day's readings are published along with the daily readings.

(5) *The award.*—A certificate is awarded for reading every day for two years, and a seal for each succeeding period of two years for eight years. Requests for these awards should be sent to the Training Union Department of the Baptist Sunday School Board, Nashville, Tennessee.

(6) *The weekly drill.*—This period of the weekly meeting may be made delightful and instructive if the Bible readers' leader will thoroughly prepare for it. It should not always be a quiz, but should often be a drill on two or three of the most interesting key verses. When questions are used, they should emphasize the outstanding teachings in the readings for the week. The leader should never use more than six to eight minutes for the drill. The following helpful suggestions are offered:

a. Sometimes drill on key verses alone, calling on various groups to give them; once in a while have the whole union give them in concert.

b. Contests of groups. A scorekeeper may be appointed and several points given for key verses quoted first, or questions answered.

c. Have members conduct drill sometimes. The Sunday before, the leader announces that each member must come prepared with a key verse or pointed question to ask. At the appointed time one member will take charge and ask one other member a question; the member answers and in turn that member asks some other member a question, and so on until the time is up.

d. The surprise drill is effective. The leader will come with prepared questions written on slips of paper. When the Bible drill is called for, the leader will call for the various members to answer the questions handed them.

e. Give favorite key verses. The Sunday before, the leader announces that each member of the union must come prepared with a favorite key verse taken from the week's readings.

f. Prepared report from timid members in the union. Once in a while the leader will ask for one-minute reports on each day's readings from different members whom the leader has privately requested to prepare and report on. This brings out the timid members.

g. Pray earnestly each day for each member of the union. Pray for the Holy Spirit to guide you, and them, into all truth. Pray for a deep and abiding love for the truth as revealed in the Word of God. Pray that each member of the union may be led to find great joy in seeking to lead the lost to Christ.

h. Commend the members for all good work done. This is very helpful.

II. THE LIBRARY AND THE BIBLE READING COMMITTEE

This is the second important phase of work committed to the Bible readers' leader. The need for good church libraries needs emphasizing greatly.

1. *Need for a Church Library*

(1) *The majority of homes do not possess many books.* —Even a casual observation, as one goes to and fro, here and there, will convince him that this statement is true to fact. It is sadly true that few homes indeed have good libraries and if the young people read good books to any great extent these books must be provided by outside agencies. Young people will read good books if they are put into their hands. Our churches, through the church libraries, ought to see that all the young people are provided with the best books available.

(2) *The majority of Baptist young people are not in reach of good libraries.*—Literally thousands of towns and villages and country communities have no public libraries, and the school libraries are limited in the number and kind of books they offer. The young people in these communities are not in reach of good books and it is idle to claim that the public libraries can supply their needs.

(3) *The influences of bad literature need to be counteracted.*—In this connection we quote a pertinent and forceful editorial in the Texas *Baptist Standard:* "We

INDIVIDUAL BIBLE READING RECORD

I Purpose

To make it a practice of my life to read the Bible and pray daily, following the plan of individual reading and private devotions of the Baptist Training Union.

Signed _____

Days of Week	1st Week	2nd Week	3rd Week	4th Week	5th Week	6th Week	7th Week	8th Week	9th Week	10th Week	11th Week	12th Week	13th Week
Sun.													
Mon.													
Tues.													
Wed.													
Thurs.													
Fri.													
Sat.													

This card may be used as a bookmark. After reading the Bible passage for the day, check in the proper square and place the card in your Bible.

FORM TU-1435-Q EIGHT POINT RECORD SYSTEM. BAPTIST SUNDAY SCHOOL BOARD NASHVILLE, TENN,
COPYRIGHT, 1951, BSSB

must counteract the influence of unclean literature. Hundreds of presses are working night and day turning out immoral books and periodicals which are being circulated by the millions through the United States mail and on newsstands. Our young people are reading this literature and their lives are being poisoned at the very time when Christian people ought to be most aggressive in disseminating the right sort of literature. We are doing very little. We have not realized the peril. Many of our homes fail to discern, and admit all sorts of literature.

"The young people are reading something; of this fact we may rest assured. There are forces at work supplying them with books and other forms of literature not fit for them to read. If any one doubts this, let him investigate the matter for himself. Let him take a glance through the magazines on the counter of any public newsstand. Even the pictures are shocking."

2. Encouraging the Reading of Good Books

The Bible reading committee of the Young People's union has two responsibilities in this connection.

(1) *Co-operate in establishing and maintaining a library.*—If the church does not have a library, the Bible reading committee should co-operate with other interested persons in helping to establish one. Leaflets giving information on the church library may be obtained free from the Church Library Service, Baptist Sunday School Board, Nashville, Tennessee.

Where a church library is already established, the Bible reading committee should make its services available periodically to help the librarian keep the library in good working condition.

(2) *Encourage the use of the library.*—At regular intervals the Bible reading committee should call attention to new books and materials which are to be found in the church library. Sometimes brief book reviews may be presented as a committee report during the time set aside for this purpose on the union schedule. (See chapter 4.)

III. THE BIBLE READERS' LEADER AND THE MONTHLY OFFICERS' COUNCIL

The Bible readers' leader should attend the monthly officers' council and help plan the work of the union. He will submit to the council, in writing, his plans for the next month. A form for this is suggested below.

The Bible readers' leader should also meet with the program committee during the first period of the general officers' council to perfect plans for Bible drills.

BIBLE READERS' LEADER'S MONTHLY REVIEW AND PLAN SHEET

.... Union

SUBMITTED TO OFFICERS' COUNCIL

For Month of..., 19....

1. Names of Bible reading committee members

   Group one ....

   Group two ....

   Group three ....

   Group four ....

2. Were assignments of work made to all these committee members the past month? ....

   What work did they report on these assignments?......................

   ....

3. Plans for next month

   (1) Plans for promotion of family altar in homes of members ....

   ....

   ....

   (2) Plans for enlistment of all members in daily Bible reading and daily prayer ....

   ....

   (3) Plans for the Bible drills for next month...........................

   ....

   ....Bible Readers' Leader

   .... Union

OUTLINE

I. THE DAILY BIBLE READERS' COURSE

    1. The Value of the Bible to the Young Christian
        (1) The Bible essential to his spiritual growth
        (2) The Bible essential to his happiness
        (3) The Bible essential to his usefulness
    2. The Purpose of the Bible Readers' Course
    3. The Place of the Bible Readers' Course
    4. The Plan of the Bible Readers' Course
    5. The Method of the Bible Readers' Course
        (1) The Bible readers' leader
        (2) Bible reading committee
        (3) Group captains
        (4) Quarterly and *Open Windows* carry Bible readers' course
        (5) The award
        (6) The weekly drill

II. THE LIBRARY AND THE BIBLE READING COMMITTEE

    1. Need for a Church Library
        (1) The majority of homes do not possess many books
        (2) The majority of Baptist young people are not in reach of good libraries
        (3) The influences of bad literature need to be counteracted
    2. Encouraging the Reading of Good Books
        (1) Co-operate in establishing and maintaining a library
        (2) Encourage the use of the library

III. THE BIBLE READERS' LEADER AND THE MONTHLY OFFICERS' COUNCIL

QUESTIONS FOR REVIEW AND EXAMINATION

FOR INSTRUCTIONS concerning the examination and the requesting of awards, see Directions for the Teaching and the Study of This Book for Credit, 129.

CHAPTER 1

1. Name three characteristics of the finished product of the Young People's union.
2. In what way does the Young People's union train for soul-winning?
3. Name five ways in which the Young People's union gives missionary training.
4. What is the responsibility of the church in developing the Young People's union?
5. Name seven things which all church members should do, and tell how the Young People's union trains them to do these things.

CHAPTER 2

6. Outline the Standard of Excellence.
7. Tell which officer is responsible for each point on the Standard of Excellence.
8. Name the officers and explain how they are elected. What is the length of the term of office?
9. What is the threefold purpose of committees?
10. Tell which officers are chairmen of committees and of which committees.
11. Tell how to divide the union into groups and appoint committees.
12. Tell how to use the Standard as the training guide.
13. What are the requirements of the Standard regarding "Achievement"?

CHAPTER 3

14. Discuss the need for department organization. (1) Where one department is needed. (2) Where two departments are needed. (3) State the purpose of the department organization.

15. Outline the work of the department director.
16. Outline the department Standard of Excellence.

CHAPTER 4

17. Tell how the president may fit himself spiritually for his work.
18. If you were elected president of a Young People's union, outline a program of work which you would attempt to carry on, as follows: (1) What would you do to prepare yourself for the work? (2) What would you try to lead the union to do?
19. Describe the work of the president and program committee, as follows: Who? When? Where? What?
20. When and how should the programs be assigned?
21. Outline a good working schedule for the president on Sunday evening.
22. When should the president hold a monthly officers' council, and what should be done in it?
23. Discuss the study course. (1) Its purpose. (2) The president's responsibility for it.
24. What is the work of the counselor?
25. Name six general lines of work for the group captain.

CHAPTER 5

26. What is the twofold work of the vice-president?
27. Describe the two classes of membership in the Young People's union.
28. Tell the sources from which names of prospects may be secured and tell how to win them to the union.
29. Tell in four points how to hold new members.
30. Tell how to win back absentees.
31. How does the Young People's union educate its members in missions?
32. What practical missionary activities may the missionary committee plan and carry on?
33. Tell how to educate and enlist the members in scriptural giving.

Chapter 6

34. Describe the threefold value of records.
35. State and explain the points in the Eight Point Record System.
36. Tell how to secure the individual report.
37. What items are reported in the secretary's record book?
38. Tell how to make the weekly report.
39. What other reports are to be made by the secretary?

Chapter 7

40. Name four duties of the social leader and the social committee.
41. What is the fellowship hour and who should sponsor it?
42. How may the social leader co-operate with the membership committee in the visitation program?

Chapter 8

43. Describe the value of the Bible to young Christians.
44. What is the purpose of the Bible readers' course?
45. Describe the plan of the Bible readers' course.
46. Give the method of the Bible readers' course in six points.
47. Discuss the work of the Bible reading committee in promoting the church library.

DIRECTIONS FOR THE TEACHING AND THE
STUDY OF THIS BOOK FOR CREDIT

I. DIRECTIONS FOR THE TEACHER

1. Ten class periods of forty-five minutes each, or the equivalent, are required for the completion of this book for credit.

2. The teacher of the class is given an award on the book if he requests it.

3. The teacher shall give a written examination covering the subject matter in the textbook, with at least one question or written assignment on each chapter, and the student shall make a minimum grade of 70 per cent. The written examination may take the form of assigned work to be done and written up between the class sessions, in the class sessions, or as a final written examination at the end of the course.

EXCEPTION: All who attend all of the class sessions; who read the book through by the close of the course; and who, in the judgment of the teacher, do the classwork satisfactorily may be exempted from taking the examination.

4. In the Graded Training Union Study Course, the Young People's diploma is granted for the completion of this book. Seal number 1 is granted for the completion of the book a second time.

Application for Training Union awards should be sent to the state Training Union department. This department will provide the form for the application. It should be made in duplicate and both copies sent.

II. DIRECTIONS FOR THE STUDENT

1. *In Classwork*

(1) The pupil must attend at least six of the ten forty-five minute class periods to be entitled to take the class examination.

(2) The pupil must certify that the textbook has been

read. (In rare cases where pupils may find it imprac-
ticable to read the book before the completion of the classwork, the teacher may accept a promise to read the book
carefully within the next two weeks.)

(3) The pupil must take a written examination, with
at least one question or written assignment from each
chapter, making a minimum grade of 70 per cent. (All who
attend all of the class sessions; who read the book through
by the close of the course; and who, in the judgment of the
teacher, do satisfactory classwork may be exempted from
taking the examination.)

2. In Individual Study by Correspondence

Those who for any reason wish to study the book without the guidance of a teacher will use one of the following
methods:

(1) Write answers to the questions printed in the book,
or
(2) Write a summary of each chapter or a development
of the chapter outlines.

If the second method is used, the student will study the
book and then with the open book write a summary of
each chapter or a development of the chapter outlines.

In either case the student must read the book through.

Students may find profit in studying the text together,
but where awards are requested, individual papers are required. (Carbon copies or duplicates in any form cannot
be accepted.) These examination papers should be mailed
to the state Training Union department.

J. E. LAMBDIN
Secretary, Training Union Department,
Baptist Sunday School Board

C. AUBREY HEARN
Director of the Study Course